D1394045

01603 773114   *Website:* studentccnac.sharepoint.com/sites/ccnlibraries
email: tis@ccn.ac.uk   🐦 @CCN_Library   📷 ccnlibrary

21 DAY LOAN ITEM

Please return <u>on or before</u> the last date stamped above

A fine will be charged for overdue items   CITY COLLEGE NORWICH

162 296

The Story of
EAST DEREHAM

An Edwardian Friendly Society or Union Procession, probably at Whitsun.

The Story of
EAST DEREHAM

Ben Norton

Illustrations by Diana Walters

Phillimore

1994

Published by
PHILLIMORE & CO. LTD.
Shopwyke Manor Barn, Chichester, Sussex

ISBN 0 85033 908 1

Printed and bound in Great Britain by
BIDDLES LTD.
Guildford, Surrey

Contents

As I meditated, a desire came strongly upon me to know what was going on in this Arcadian paradise—and I could find no rest till I had gone some way toward reconstructing the little community and bringing it to life again. But it is idle and foolish to give the reins to Imagination unless Fact acts as a charioteer and holds the ribbons. So I went to my documents and the past came back at my call, gradually peopled with living forms that rose about me, the dry bones stirring, 'bone to his bone', and the flesh mysteriously growing round the skeletons, and men and women standing up and staring at me, 'a very great army'.

AUGUSTUS JESSOPP DD
1823-1914

List of Illustrations

Frontispiece: An Edwardian procession, Market Place.

Acknowledgements

Many kind friends have helped us to bring out this book.

We are deeply indebted to David Walters for his invaluable computer expertise in preparing the typescript and for his unstinted support throughout.

The foundations were laid by Christopher Barringer during his excellent three-year course on our local history arranged jointly by the Dereham branch of the Workers' Educational Association and the University of Cambridge Board of Extra-Mural Studies. The Dereham W.E.A. have subsequently given us much help and encouragement.

Susan Palmer provided much useful material, including the 'Old Coucher' and many photographs. Joyce Dixon also loaned several fine photographs. Mr David J.M. Armstrong kindly allowed us to make use of his great-grandfather's diaries, and the Rev. J.B. Boston permitted the use of material from *Dereham, The Biography of a Country Town*. Canon Dennis Rider has agreed to the use of the East Dereham Churchwardens' Accounts and Eastern Counties Newspapers have kindly allowed us to quote extensively from the *Norfolk Chronicle*, and we are also grateful for the fine foreword written by John Timpson, who obviously appreciates Dereham as much as we do.

We have also used short quotations from many sources, including the BBC television programme *Civilisation*, George Borrow, Thomas Hardy, Rudyard Kipling, Arthur Lee-Warner, Charles Loftus, Canon Macnaughton Jones, Thomas Munnings, Siegfried Sassoon, H.W. Saunders, C.H. Wollaston and Parson Woodforde.

We made extensive use of the facilities provided by the Norfolk Record Office, the Local Studies Department of the Norwich Central Library and the Dereham Library. We are grateful to the staff concerned for their courteous assistance.

Preface

George Carthew started it. He was a local solicitor, churchwarden and antiquarian, who in 1855 gave a lecture entitled 'The Town we live in' at the newly opened Mechanics Institute. It was well received, and with some embellishments was later published under the title *The History of East Dereham*. This was the first attempt to reveal the town's past. Carthew's excellent researches have been the foundation of our local histories ever since; to adapt a well-known couplet:

> Dereham, and Dereham's past lay hid in night,
> God said 'Let Carthew be' and all was light.

Next, Canon Macnaughton-Jones, vicar of Dereham, published a book in 1929 with the title, East *Dereham, Its Historical and Archaeological Features with Illustrations*. Despite its grandiloquent title it was a very small book which disposed of the town's history, apart from the parish church, in about two thousand words—this book is now out of print.

In 1952 along came Boston and Puddy. They were not a music hall act, though—come to think of it—tall austere Dr. E. Ivimy Puddy and rotund, rubicund Canon Noel Boston might have become the Morecambe and Wise of the 1950s if they had put their minds to it. Instead they produced a book, *East Dereham, The Biography of a Country Town*, which is the definitive history of Dereham, and very good it is. Unfortunately, it too is out of print and copies are hard to come by.

And so, to fill this void, this book has been compiled. It makes no claim to academic merit or original research, and borrows much material from sources now out of print so as to produce something worthwhile. It would be shameful if the 'genius loci' was left in limbo crying out for form and substance.

To those men whose names are carved
on our War Memorial

Foreword

When a town changes so dramatically in size and character in the space of thirty or forty years, it is invaluable to have a permanent record of what it used to be like. Ben Norton has written a very thoroughly researched history of Dereham, a town which I remember with great affection from my days on the *Dereham & Fakenham Times* in the 1950s, but which I confess I now tend to avoid. It has become too much like the very towns which I came to Norfolk to escape from ...

I am sure that even Dereham's newer residents are familiar with the legend of St Withburga, and know about the town's connections with George Borrow and William Cowper, but there is much else to be learned about Dereham's past, even by those born and bred there. This new history fills in any gaps which may have been left by Canon Boston and Dr. Puddy in the book they wrote during my own days in the town.

That book of course ended the story in the 1950s, and Mr. Norton chooses to end his in the same period, on the day in 1950 when the statue of Coke of Norfolk on the roof of the Corn Hall (which I remember better as the Exchange Cinema) was struck by lightning and knocked off its plinth. 'It was a delightfully symbolic incident,' he writes. 'Soon after that, the cattle market was closed and the town eschewed its solid old agricultural heritage.'

Well, not immediately. I came to Dereham in 1951, and during my eight years on the paper (which was not the *East Dereham & Fakenham Times*, so Dereham has always been Dereham to me) it was still a peaceful, unspoilt market town, with a special character all its own. I wrote later:

> Newsgathering was a joy in this kind of world, where a walk across the Market Place could take half an hour, as I paused for a chat here and a word or two there. Over a pint in the *King's Arms* I could pick up enough ideas to fill a couple of columns, and in the cattle market on a Friday I could fill a couple more. It all took a little time, because there are a lot of pauses in Norfolk conversations, considerable periods of contemplation and silent thought, and often I impetuously chipped in with another question as the minutes ticked by, only to receive a continuation of the answer to the previous one ...

Those days, alas, have long since gone. A leisurely stroll across the Market Place today would be suicidal. There is no room on the pavements to stop and chat, even if you could find a Norfolkman to chat to. And soon after I left, the *King's Arms* was demolished to make way for Woolworths. To me, that was the real beginning of the end of the old Dereham.

And what of the new? It is described diplomatically on the cover of Mr. Norton's book as a 'bright, bustling modern town', and no doubt that is the way many people see it, but I am relieved to find that Mr. Norton himself shares my own sadness at the way it is developing into what he calls 'yet another Admassville'.

All the more, then, that we should have a book such as this, to remind us that it was not ever thus.

JOHN TIMPSON, OBE

JUNE 1994

Chapter I

654 and All That

East Dereham owes its genesis to a princess, a miracle—and milk. The princess was Withburga, loveliest of all the Saxon saints, who came to this spot to found a nunnery, but the death in battle of her father, King Anna of the East Angles, in A.D. 654, left her destitute. The miracle happened when, left with only dry bread to feed her nuns and workmen, she prayed long and hard for help. Afterwards she fell into a slumber, in which she saw the Queen of Virgins, adorned with inexpressible beauty and majesty, who bid her put her confidence in God and not trouble herself for the morrow: 'Send', she said, 'early in the morning your maids to the neighbouring bridge over the stream and there shall meet them every day two does whose milk shall minister to your necessities'.

And so the nunnery was built and here Withburga lived out her blameless days until, in the words of an old commemorative service, 'she was raised with the palm of virginity to the courts of heaven'. Make what you will of this old legend, one thing is certain: East Dereham was a place of some importance and a name in the pages of history at a very, very early date.

The nunnery was probably only a small place, for no trace of it has ever been found. Indeed, archaeological remains of any sort are surprisingly sparse in Dereham. A few bits and pieces from prehistoric times have been dug up, but nothing to throw light on our medieval past is officially recorded. There was, however, an interesting item in the *Dereham and Fakenham Times* a year or so back, supplied by Mr. Eric Cave, son of a photographer whose shop was in Church Street. The floor of this shop collapsed in 1934. 'We found out that at one time there had been a monastery all along there', Mr. Cave said. 'Underneath the floor were all the little niches where the monks used to sleep.' This sounds very intriguing and one day these remains may perhaps be seen again and given expert examination. However, it seems unlikely that monks slept in niches underground; a medieval wine cellar, perhaps?

Small as it was, the nunnery did not escape the attentions of the Danish raiders of A.D. 870. Along with rich abbeys and great churches it was looted and destroyed. The virgin sisterhood were driven out, and the words of the old monk who recorded the event, 'fugato virginum cetum in parochiam ut destitutum', were freely translated by Mr. Carthew as 'they became chargeable to the parish'.

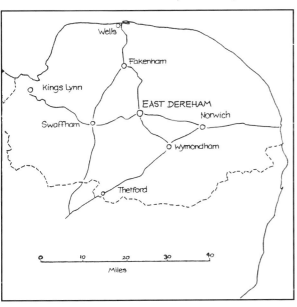

1   The position of East Dereham in Norfolk.

1

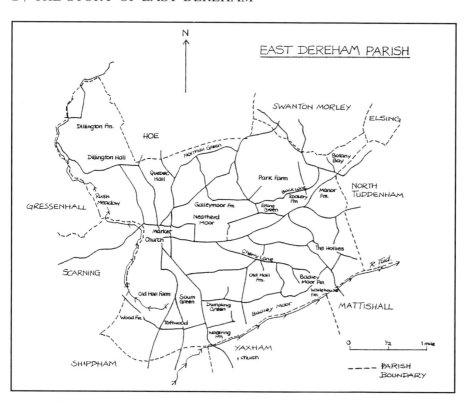

2 The parish of East Dereham.

This was the end of the nunnery, but the church was rebuilt as the parish church. It contained the shrine of St Withburga, which became a great attraction for pilgrims and brought riches to the little community.

Later, in 970, King Edgar of England bestowed the manor of East Dereham on the abbey of Ely and a great change took place in the fortunes of the town. In an act of astonishing callousness and insensitivity the abbot removed St Withburga's venerated body to his abbey. Ostensibly it was to give her a more suitable shrine in a large church; actually it was to secure for his Ely coffers the rich gifts of the pilgrims. This robbery has given rise to many a fine story, but briefly it was accomplished thus:

3 St Withburga's well.

4 Abbot of Ely with the body of St Withburga on the way from Brandon to Ely.

In 974 the Abbot, as lord of the manor, visited the town and held his manor court, after which he gave a sumptuous feast for all the town, being careful to provide a plentiful supply of strong drink. After this carousal the good people of the town were ready for bed, and one by one retired.

The time was ripe for the abbot to put into execution a plan, drawn up with great precision. St Withburga's body was removed from her tomb and put on a carriage standing ready. Accompanied by the abbot's retainers, the cortège moved off by road to Brandon where boats were ready and waiting to complete the journey by river. By this time the enraged Dereham people had caught them up, but having no boats of their own could only run along the river bank and let fly a barrage of stones—let us hope that a well-aimed stone raised a large bump on the shaven pate of that infamous abbot.

One version of the story added a touch of magic to this sordid robbery, when the chronicler recorded that:

> They were accompanied during their whole journey thither by a very bright star which shone upon the virgin's body and emitted bright rays.

A fuller account of this legend appears in Appendix I of this book.

So the town was left to face a bleak future without its beloved saint. All chances of becoming the major religious focus of the region (which it so thoroughly deserved to be) had gone. Today, crowds pour into Walsingham during the pilgrimage season, many passing through Dereham. How many stop to think that this place was old and sacred when Walsingham was only a cluster of peasants' huts? Fortunately one remembrance of Withburga was left. A well had formed in the site of her original burial; its waters gained a reputation for healing qualities, and pilgrims were once again attracted to the town. This, together with a market founded by royal charter, seems to have helped to retain some prosperity in the place. Church Street, much too wide to have been just a medieval street, is thought to be the site of the Saxon market. Certainly, well into this century it was used as an extension of the cattle market, and had iron posts along the pavement, similar to those still standing at the top of the market place. These posts used to form the corner posts for cattle pens on market days.

When the Normans came, following the invasion in 1066, they evidently found a thriving community, for a new church was built which seems to have been an imposing building. Very little is left today; the south doorway of the present church is a fine example of Norman work, Norman shafts have been built into the chancel arch and fragments of Norman masonry are scattered about the chancel walls. Experts have examined these remains and, as experts invariably do, they disagreed over their significance, but it seems reasonable to conclude that this old Norman church was no mean building. The mystery is, what became of it? A hundred or so years later, in the 13th century, a new church in the Early English style was built. Perhaps the old one was destroyed by fire, or perhaps it just fell down for Norman church building was notoriously a hit and miss affair.

5 St Nicholas' door

The Early English 13th-century church was enlarged and added to at various times right up to the early 16th century when the detached bell tower, or 'clocker' was built. The legend usually attached to such separate towers is that the devil, being allergic to church bells, tried to make off with the tower, but being disturbed was forced to drop it. Since we can say with confidence that 'Old Nick' would never dare show his horns in our parish, the explanation given here is different, and the story as told by an old sexton is recorded by R.H. Mottram in his book, *East Anglia*:

> The explanation given me of the separate bell-tower, runs differently from that in most guide books. The old sexton I asked spoke as follows:
>
> 'That tower, that used to be joined ont' th' church, only the chap what built it, he never put in the mortar, same as he should ha' done, he jus' shoved any ole muck inter that mortar, so that was never watertight. Rain used t' come right thro' that, till that was wringing wet. Then, the ole Rector, he got right sick an' tired o' that, so he say: "D'yew get some tar, and tar that tower all over, that'll keep that dry!"
>
> 'So they done like what he said. Only, the day they done that, while that tar was all sticky, and not set like, here come a whole flock o' young starlings, and they flittered and they fluttered, all over the tower where that was tarred, an' the more they stuck, the more duller [douleur or commotion], they made, and with all them young b'ds a-fluttering together, they fluttered the tower off the church to where that stand now. Corse, that took some time, and the tar, that dried and then they fluttered theirselves loose!'
>
> 'O come, I don't believe that!', I replied.
>
> 'Dont yew?' he responded. 'Then haow d'yew reckon that got where it is?'

6   The church tower.

The tower was left where the birds dropped it, which enabled it to be put to good use during the Napoleonic Wars as a lock-up for French prisoners-of-war being marched from Yarmouth to the prison at Norman Cross. One such prisoner, a nimble French lieutenant, Jean de Narde, contrived to escape and made off, pursued with alacrity by a sentry—the prospect of several hundred lashes across one's bare back can generate a remarkable amount of alacrity! He took refuge up a tree, and refused to come down when challenged, whereupon he was 'shot out of the tree like a crow'. He was buried in the churchyard, and later our notable

7   Memorial cross in Dereham churchyard, erected in 1857 by Rev. B.J. Armstrong to commemorate the death in 1799 of Jean de Narde.

19th-century vicar, the Rev. B.J. Armstrong, moved by this sad story had a stone put on his grave. It stands today, inscribed:

> In Memory of Jean de Narde, son of a notary public of St. Malo.
>
> A French Prisoner of War who having escaped from the Bell Tower of this church was pursued and shot by a soldier on duty October 6th 1799. Aged 28 years.
>
> This memorial of his untimely fate has been erected by the Vicar and two friends who accompanied him in a visit to Paris as a tribute of respect to that brave and generous nation once our foes but now our Allies and brethren.
>
> Ainsi soit il
>
> A.D. 1857.

To revert to 1066: the coming of the Normans does not appear to have brought undue hardship to the town. The abbot of Ely was diplomatic enough to keep on reasonably good terms with King William and was permitted to retain his lands. Less fortunate was Archbishop Stigand, whose properties at Dillington passed to a Norman, William de Beaufoe.

In 1086 came the Domesday Survey, beloved of historians but perhaps less meaningful to the average reader. We are indebted to Mr. Carthew for setting out in readable form the details for Dereham:

> Referring to this survey, we find that the quantity of land under the plough in King Edward's time, viz., about the middle of the 11th century, in what may be called Dereham proper, was about 1,200 acres, of which about 240 were held in hand by the monastery, and cultivated under the superintendence of their own bailiff, and about 960 were in the hands of tenants—not tenants in the present sense of the term, who are free to give up their occupations when they please, and move where they please; but men attached to the soil from which they derived their maintenance, and who were bought and sold with it, having this privilege, which the mere serf had not, they could not be sold or removed at the pleasure of their lord from the land they dwelt upon;—of these, called villeins, there were 20, and there were twenty other occupiers called bordars, whose exact position in the social scale is not fully understood, but I believe they cultivated the lord's land, and held

8 St Withburga's church.

small occupations on the terms of furnishing corn, meat, and fowls for the lord's board or table.

There were also three mills on the estate; and there was sufficient quantity of woodland left to afford support for 600 swine (a considerable source of wealth to our Saxon ancestors) from the acorns upon which they chiefly subsisted, besides the pasturage afforded by the heaths and meadow grounds. In addition to the dwellers before mentioned, were seven socmen, a more independent class of tenants, who held among them thirty acres of arable land, two of meadow and three of wood. Thus the population of Dereham connected with the land 900 years ago, consisted of thirty seven families only, which averaging five in a family, would be one hundred and eighty-five persons. [Mr Carthew was undoubtedly an astute lawyer, but he was not so good at simple arithmetic. He should have said 'forty-seven families —two hundred and thirty-five persons'.] This indeed, included the profitable class only; there were the Abbot's bailiff with his family and servants; the clergymen and theirs; but even with these additions, Hoe and Dillington, together had a larger population than Dereham proper. In that district which lay in the Hundred of Launditch, also called Dereham in Domesday Book, and which I consider comprised Dillington and so much of Hoe as was not within the Abbey domain, were four villeins, fifteen bordars and two serfs. The lord had about two hundred and forty acres under the plough; and the tenants the same quantity; there was wood enough to feed thirty swine, and five socmen held forty three acres of arable land and two acres of meadow. These were part of the possession of Stigand, who had been Bishop of the East Angles, and at the Conquest was Archbishop of Canterbury. The Abbot's territory in Hoe was inhabited by eight villeins and ten bordars, who cultivated about three hundred and sixty acres of arable land, and eight of meadow, besides about one hundred and twenty acres under the plough, kept for the Abbot's own use. There was wood enough for one hundred swine, and one mill. There were, also, two socmen who held twenty four acres of arable land and four of meadow, and wood enough for four swine. So the population of Hoe and Dillington together, being at least forty six families, may be estimated to have been, before the Norman Conquest, as much as at the present day.

Chapter II
Tranquil Distant Years

And so we come to the late Middle Ages, a remarkable period in the town's history—a period for which we have very little recorded history. Four hundred years passed in a state of delicious uneventfulness under the benign and efficient administration of the Church. In the absence of any notable events we can only picture the inhabitants passing the years engaged in wholesome but unremarkable pastoral pursuits and handing on the torch of Life from generation to generation. It was the world epitomised by Thomas Hardy:

> Only a man harrowing clods
> In a slow silent walk
> With an old horse that stumbles and nods
> Half asleep as they stalk.
>
> Only thin smoke without flame
> From the heaps of couch-grass;
> Yet this will go onward the same
> Though Dynasties pass.
>
> Yonder a maid and her wight
> Come whispering by:
> War's annals will cloud into night
> Ere their story die.

In 1251 Bishop Hugh de Northwold had a survey made of all his manors, known sometime as the 'Old Coucher' or Liber R. The administration of a medieval manor was carried on in accordance with the unwritten 'Custom of the Manor' which depended for definition on the memories of the oldest inhabitants. Understandably, there was much wrangling in the manor courts between the lord and his serfs when any changes in working conditions were proposed. It must have been rather like today's interminable negotiations between trade unions and management. And so, to define the manorial customs beyond dispute, the survey was made. It was a masterpiece of thoroughness and precise detail; recording every half farthing of rent due, all the customary works which his unfree tenants had to provide down to the last six inches of fencing round the park, and every half egg due to the bishop at Easter. Half an egg!—presumably they boiled one and sliced it in two.

Boston and Puddy had access to this document when writing their history of Dereham and made certain comments on it, but they did not go into detail. Wisely perhaps, for it is an unwieldy and repetitive mass of material to handle. Even so, since it offers such a unique glimpse of everyday life in the parish at a time when so little is otherwise known, we have included sufficient selections in Appendix IV to cover the most important aspects. It is a document of great interest to the specialist and the student of the administration of medieval manors; the average reader will not be censured for skipping it! It begins:

9 Plough.

Dereham

The Inquisition made by Richard, son of Matthew, John Le Frere, William de Massingham, Ralph at the Church Gate, clerk, Nicholas Odeline, William Hackesalt, Ralph de Humbletoft, Henry de Northal, Adam Husebonde and John son of Ralph de Northal, Ralph Treye, Ralph Kyde, Symon Mammang, Ralph de Hil, Richard de Franceis, Adam son of William, John Rodewi, Robert Ulf, Thomas le Neueman of Jakesham, Robert Lefsy, Richard Aleman, Richard Maydewyn, William Sunelles, William ate Ryde, John de Bylneye, Peter Brun, Ralph de Sathale, Warin at the Bridge, Adam Husebond of Ho and John Crabbe of Ho.

This manor is in the county of Norfolk and in the Hundred of Midford, which is the free hundred of the Lord Bishop of Ely—except the street of Northale which is in the hundred of Laundick, which is John le Strange's of Ludham and in which hundred the men dwelling in the same street assemble at Strutemannesdich once in the year for the renewal of their pledges. And then, in the presence of the Bailiff of the hundred and of the Bailiff of the Lord Bishop, they make fine of 2s that they may not be disturbed, whereof the Bailiff of the Bishop shall have 20d and the Bailiff of that hundred 4d by the hand of the clerk of the Bishop's Bailiff or he shall eat with him at the charge of the Bishop.

The advowson and donation of the Church together with the Chapel of Ho belongs to the Bishop of Ely and is in the Bishopric of Norwich; but be it known that the said Church is in the Archdeanery of Norfolk and in the deanery of Hengham, and the said Chapel of Ho is in the Archdeanery of Norwich and in the deanery of Brusele.

(See Appendix IV for the remaining excerpts.)

The survey goes on to define the bishop's desmesne. This was his own land which he cultivated, or rather was cultivated for him 'By the boon and customary works of the town'.

Hugh de Northwold has been described as 'the good monk bishop'; but perhaps he was also the high-farming bishop *par excellence* in the history of the bishopric of Ely, simply because he was a monk in days when the monastic order was 'the nurse of intelligent and broad-minded landowners'. When he died in 1254 his successors proved less keen on agriculture, preferring instead to be rentiers, and so by about 1286 most of the Dereham demesne had been leased, much to the relief, no doubt, of Ralph de Humbletoft and those like him who had been compelled to work the demesne in addition to their own lands.

There was one customary work, though, which may well have been welcomed. That of 'carrying on foot or with horse and sack', an important and necessary task in the scattered possessions of the bishop. By this service one manor could assist another in times of shortage, produce could be sent to the bishop's household at Ely, and when the bishop was engaged in his frequent visitations supplies could be sent to sustain his considerable entourage. The destinations mentioned included Schypedham, Bregham, Feltwelle, Northwande, Hockwande and Pulham, which were the bishop's manors. Norwich and Lynn were also included: Norwich was important for its market and Lynn was a seaport where necessaries for the manorial economy could be purchased. In old records building timber, oil and pitch for the shepherd are mentioned, as well as common foodstuffs and medieval luxuries—figs and raisins, almonds, pepper and ginger, nuts and sugar, honey and wine, salmon and porpoises. Brandon Bridge is listed; this was the embarkation point for traffic to Ely by water. It was along this route that poor Withburga had been carried with her star hovering over her; and behind streamed the

10 11th-century costume.

people of Dereham in panting but futile pursuit. These expeditions must have provided a pleasant break in the humdrum life of a manorial worker, with a chance to see the world outside the parish boundaries.

Over 300 tenants were listed in the survey; using Mr. Carthew's average of five persons per family gives a population of 1,500; in addition there would be landless men and squatters. At that time the population of London was 50,000 and Norwich, the second city, 10,000. Dereham was evidently no mean town for those days.

Most of the men's Christian names were simple and are familiar today. Richard (38) was the favourite, William and Ralph tied for second place at 32 each and Robert came third with 27. John (19), Adam (14), Henry and Roger (12 each) and Hugh (11) were also popular. Names like Warin and Odo are out of fashion now. A few ladies' names were listed: Agnes, Alice, Emma and Margaret for example, again familiar today.

Surnames were not universal; when shown they were frequently derived from 'place' names like Andrew de Acre, William Docking, John de Bylney or Thomas de Hereford (who did not come from Hereford but from the manor of that name in 'Ho'). There were also 'trade' names—Richard Baker, Ralph Carpenter or William Smith. Other familiar names were Richard Starling, Richard Spink and Geoffry Dunning, but some surnames sound rather outlandish—Robert Flur, Walter Fle, Warin Pie and Roger Rot. When a man had no surname the biblical method was adopted—Adam son of William, Geoffrey son of Symon or John son of Robert.

It is rather intriguing to find the name Odo ate Stile in Dereham in 1251, for the Elizabethan muster roll three hundred years later contains the name Martyne at Style. We also had Little Martin and Adam the smith's son —they would have been welcome in Sherwood, Robert le Fay, on the other hand suggests connections with the court of King Arthur!

The parish today extends over 5,000 acres, and its boundaries would presumably have been much the same in 1251. The survey shows about 2,500 acres under cultivation or as messuages, which leaves as much again to be accounted for.

The Park and Toftwood together contained 230 acres, and the town and market must be taken into account. Part of the remaining 2,000 odd acres would have been the commons and wastes. At the time of the 1815 Enclosure Act these commons contained about 850 acres, so evidently there had been a good deal of 'assarting' (the clearing and cultivation of woodland and waste) going on over the intervening period. The details given under 'Of those new infeofed' include examples of this existing practice by men who had carved for themselves little holdings out of virgin land and who therefore had no customary services to render. But there is also the question of the other manors in the parish, whose origins are obscure (see page 18). Perhaps they account for some of the surplus land.

It is interesting to read, under the heading 'Of the turbery' early in the survey, the phrase 'the whole soke of Dereham'. A soke was a supra-manorial unit based upon extensive commons in which a number of villages had joint rights, and the survey shows how this inter-commoning was carried out. This does suggest that the commons in this area were unusually large. Most of the names recorded almost 750 years ago are recognisable today:

Estlingker common (Badley moor)
Etlinge green
Southwode green (Dumpling green)
Brunesmor common (?Toftwood common)
Morgate green (South green)
Buckmede (Rush Meadow)
Northalegreen (Northall green)
Galewetremor (Neatherd)

And so, when we walk on the Neatherd or Etling Green we are walking on common land which has changed little for probably a thousand years.

However we should beware of taking all the figures of acreage and extent at face value, since in those days some of the measurements in use were rather elastic. A virgate, for example, might contain 20 to 30 acres or more; for these calculations we have assumed it to be 25 acres. A perch was sometimes 16½ and sometimes 20 feet. Even an acre could vary; you will notice the demesne is reckoned at 358½ acres 'by the little hundred', and in some instances in the Ely survey as a whole 'ware acres' were used to measure villein holdings and 'field acres' for the demesne. A ware acre was equal to 1½, or in some cases 2, field acres.

11 14th-century farm-workers.

Complete accuracy is not important: what is important is that this survey pulls back the veil of the years and we are privileged to catch a glimpse of 'a fair field full of folk' living and working here all those years ago in what appears to be comfortable and pleasant circumstances. We can even learn the names of some of our forefathers who would otherwise have lived and died in complete obscurity. It also shows what extensive powers the Bishop could wield over his lands. The hundred of Mitford was almost an independent state within the kingdom and the king's officials were kept at arm's length. The bishop had his own prison and gallows; his own court and coroner; the right of free warren (i.e. hunting and sporting rights) and many other priviliges.

It is awful to think that this peaceful community, in 100 years time, 1349, would be reduced to half its size by the most terrible calamity ever to strike our country—the Black Death which carried off the vicar, William de Sutlee, and an unknown number of his parishioners. Nationwide the mortality was terrible; between one third and a half of the population is one estimate. This meant, of course, a grave shortage of labour and much discontent among the surviving peasants who thought it about time that the old ways were changed. In course of time changes did come; the old system of service to the lord was replaced by payments called free rents and quit rents.

Dereham at the end of the Middle Ages seems to have been a prosperous place; no doubt much money was made from the wool trade. There were no less than 16 guilds attached to the church, and guilds usually indicated wealth. George Carthew referred to them in that famous lecture of 18 April 1855, when light was first shed on the town's past:

These Wills make mention of several guilds, which were societies whose objects were much the same as those designed by modern benefit clubs,- mutual charity and good fellowship,—but with these they combined pious provisions for religious services, and for this purpose each guild had its own altar in the parish church, and often built an additional aisle or chapel to it: we have two such in our own church.

Hence also, they had their own guildhalls, in which the affairs of their business were discussed and settled, and where their social meetings, for relaxation and the interchange of good feeling, were held. Each of these societies was called after the name of its patron saint; and besides the annual subscriptions of the members, they were often endowed with donations of land and, as we have seen, by legacies. It was quite as much in consequence of these endowments, as of the superstitious uses to which they were applied, that these fraternities were abolished by the Council which governed the realm in the name of Edward VI, when their possessions were forfeited by virtue of an act of parliament obtained for that purpose. As we know the site of the Hall which had belonged to one of these guilds, it will not be irrelevant to this Lecture to mention it. The guild of St. Withburga had a guidhall, and 18 acres of land belonging to it, which in 1548, were sold and granted by the Crown to Thomas Wodehouse, Esq., and by him to William Skarlett, of this place.

Traces of the orginal building can be seen in the wall of the present day Guildhall.

Other guilds mentioned by Blomefield were: St Mary, St Mary Magdalen, Corpus Christi, Holy Cross, St Peter, Holy Trinity, St George, St Thomas, St Margaret, St Catherine, St James, St Michael and Jesu. These were in existence in 1458. The will of Thomas Spyrk, dated 1474, mentions in addition St Anne and St Nicholas.

The chapels and altars referred to by Carthew were dealt with at length by Boston and Puddy. They concluded that the chapel of the Blessed Virgin was in the south transept, the altar of St John was where the clergy vestry now is, St Peter's Chapel either against the screen at the east end of the south aisle, or against the next screen immediately south of the chapel of St John; the altar of St Cross was either immediately below the lantern tower or in the centre of the second crossing imediately to its east; St Thomas of

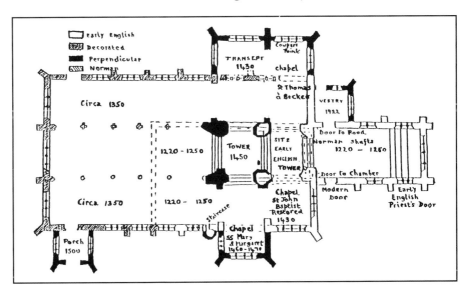

12 Plan of St Nicholas' church.

13 Washbridge, with St Nicholas' church in the background, c.1936.

Canterbury's altar would occupy the position of the present northern chapel and St Edmund's altar would be against the screen to the west of this chapel; St Withburga's chapel would be at the site of the well and its ruins are the walls which surround the well.

The Pre-Reformation church must have presented a wonderful picture, with the lights on the guild altars twinkling; rich colouring and statues all round and the constant coming and going of the guild chaplains and members.

Chapter III

'Defaste with Fire'

The 16th century brought great changes. First came the Reformation which does not seem to have affected Dereham too harshly, except for the loss of the chantries and the guilds. One major change did take place, though. In the first year of her reign, Queen Elizabeth indulged in a bit of land-grabbing and among her acquisitions was the bishop's manor of East Dereham. She persuaded him to hand it over— he was a wise bishop in acquiescing to this, since Queen Elizabeth had considerable powers of persuasion, not least among them being the rack and the block. Dereham then became known as 'Dereham of the Queen'.

Then came the threat of the Armada, and men were called up for military service—'musters', as they were called. The records compiled in connection with these musters are very interesting. For a second time we get lists of names of local people, some of which are familiar in the town today.

MITFORDE HUNDRED

East Dereham

Hacquebutts
Selected archers
Ralfe Chmney
William Futtour gent
Richard Thomson
Jamys Sheringhm
Anthony Cobb
Robert Chymney
Henry Blanche
John Harryson
Wyllm Trenche
Thoms Clere
Wyllm Wylkenson
John Gerfe
Ralfe Pepp
George Mollyn
Wyllm Owlys
Willm Sands
Thoms Byrchm
John Brown Jun
Anthony White
John Gallant
Wyllm Stokken
Hugh Poynter
John Skarff

Thoms Murton
Powle Michell
John Owtlawe

Hacquebutters selectyd
Edm Owtlawe
Jamys Lane
Francs Wells
Peter Deye
Wyllm Batles
Wyllm Stanhowe
Thoms Geffreys
Richard Rack
John Walle

Pykemen
Jeremy Kyng
Roger Wells
Geffrey Frost
Robert Drane
Edmond Moultyng
Francs Flower
Edward Gurney
Richard Atlee
John Martyn
John Clerk
John Bache

Pykemen Selectyd
Arthure Legate
John Curteys
Rowland Crane
Robert Clerk
Willm Edwards
Richard Malster
Robert Ferrour
Thoms Wells

Archers
Robert Byrde
John Smyth
John Bulward
Wyllm Ryse
Wyllm Shynne
Edmond Michell
Thoms Byrchm
Mathew Wylson
Thoms Croche
Robert Pynnes
Robert Barrett
Vyncent Duck
John Carre
Anthony Star
John Gough
Wyllm Payn't
John Harvye

Hugh Vinmok
John Woods
Thom Starling
John Flower

Bylmen

Dennys Yonges
John Briges
Wyllm Mowtyng
Robert Taylor
Edmond Burde
Edmond Combye
John Leaks ye elder
Robert Batche
Edmond Bell
John Fresshwater
Robert Fissher
Wyllm Machyn
Richard Meltram
Robert Shortyng
John Wynde
John Peckett
Symon Studde
George Croche
Wyllm Cross
Robert Neale
Nicholas Mynnes
Wyllm Awgar
Thoms Pynnes

John Wright
Anthony Duckett
Nicholas Perrymont
Wyllm Rockeslye
Roger Pecock
Nicholas Amyas
Martyne AtStyle
Robert Lawse
John Wylson
Thomas Woodhouse
John Jeye
Thomas Romm
John Shynkgnyn
Edward Hall
Thomas Lambert
Wyllm Shortyng
Richard Lancastre
John Johnson
Matthew Deye
John Carter
Henry Case
Thoms Trench
Wyllm Woffytt
Thoms Hurrell
Leond Vynsent
Wyllm Bealys Jun
Jamys Archer
Francs Rysing
Henry Mego

Wyllm Bealys sen
John Reade Jun
Charles Reade
Edmond Newton
John Coote
Richard Abll +
    John Wenne
John Burges
Wyllm Clubbe
Clement Pomfrett
Gregory Patrick
Thoms Harryson

Smythes

Ralfe Perry
Stevyne Forman
John Barton
Peter Deye
Pyons & Laborers
Thoms Marshall
John Leake
Pcyvall Symson
John Olyver
George Bencher
Richard Dethick
Willm Smyth
George Brinkley

MITFORD HUNDRED

THE BOOKE OF the armour within the hundred of Mitford seen & viewed at the generall Musters taken at Wyndham common the XVth Day of Auguste., in the XIXth yere of the reyne of our Soverane lady Queen Elyzabeth, As well as of suche Armor shotte munytion and artillery as every person within the sayd Hundred is charged withall by Vertue of the statut in suche case made & provided. As allso of all supply of armor, weapon and shott incresed & had in redynes by the inhabitants within the sayed hundred as ensueth.

ESTDERHAM
The township there

one Corselett
ij Calyvers   } by supplye
one bowe

Richard Atlee
one Allmayne Revett } by statute
And one bowe

the same Richard
one Calyv.   by supply

Henry Moulting gent
one Almayne Revet
one bowe   } by statute
one Calyver

Wyllm Futter gent
one bowe   by statute
& one Calyver   by supply

Wyllm Stannowe gent
one Calvyer   by supply

Richard Racke
  one Calyver   by supply
  - Ixford
  one bowe   by statute

the same
  John Marshall &
  Thomas Dallton   } by supply
  one Corselett

Richard Dethick
  one almayne Revett } by
  & one bowe   } statute

Hugh Poynter
  one bowe by statute

The same Hugh &
Stefen Forman   } by supply
  one Calyver

Arthur Skarlett gent
  one Calyver   by supply

Nicolas Crosman gent
  one Calyver   by supply

Arthur Legat gent
  one Corselett   by supply

John Smyth
  one bowe   by supply

Willm Beales tayler
  one bowe   by supply

Henry Skarlett
  one bowe   by supply

John Bryges
  one bill
  one sallett   by supply

Roger Wills
  one bill

Willm Moulting
  one bill
  one sworde
  & a dagger

James Sheringham
  one bowe & a   } by supply
  shefe of arrows

Robert Chymney
  ij bills

Robert Rudd
  ———

Robert Fisher
  one bill & sallett

Rafe Peper
  one bill & sallett

Edmund Michell
  a bowe

Willm Shorting
  Hallfe a shefe of
  arrows

Willm Rowse
  one bowe & a
  shefe of arrowes

Hugh Womak
  one bowe & a
  shefe of arrowes

Sum of :
  Corseletts iij
  Calyvers x
  bowes xiiij
  Allmayn Revetts iij
  bills vij

The troops stood ready to repel the invaders with a motley collection of weapons (but which the 1940 Home Guard would have envied), but it was not the Armada beacons that stained the sky over Dereham one fateful July night. An enemy within had struck with ruthless ferocity. It was the great fire of Dereham which broke out on Tuesday, 18 July 1581. A Dereham man, Arthur Gurney, witnessed it and wrote a poem entitled 'A Doleful Discourse and Ruthfull Report of the great Spoyle and loss by Fire in the Towne of East Dereham'. It goes on for 96 verses and though it maunders on somewhat about the wickedness of man and the rightness of God's punishment, it also contains some vivid descriptions of the scene at the height of the blaze. The second and third verses of this poem, quoted below, give us a valuable glimpse of the standing of 16th-century Dereham—a picture of a small but happy community.

> A Towne I was though blest, not brave, God wott,
> Ne of renoune, my name was allwayes small,

> My treasures thinne, yet trades which I had gott,
> Did hould me high upon an happy stall;
> An ayde was I, but in no case a thrall,
> To neighbour Townes dispersed here and there,
> My state was sound and stoode for stately chere.
> My fields full faire, my pastures pight for good,
> My waters cleare, my fruict sufficient:
> My bounds both broade and well bestad with wood,
> My commons large and comly to content.

(The rest of what remains of this poem is printed in Appendix II.)

The fire broke out after a month of heat and drought. It seems to have started in Church Street, and a south-west wind drove the flames into the market place, after which it veered west and then to the north-west. 52 tenements and 350 'houses of office' were destroyed, the damage done being estimated at £14,000. The 1811 census showed 567 houses for a population of 2,888, and this included the outlying hamlets. The 1581 population was probably only about half that, and 402 houses would suggest almost complete devastation. Medieval Dereham vanished overnight like the mythical Brigadoon. The church survived to stand like the Rock of Ages over the ruins, to give heart to the stricken community, and, ironically, so did Bishop Bonner's cottage. That infamous bishop was so associated with unspeakable atrocities by fire, that the local name for the ladybird, 'bishybarnabee', is said to be a corruption of 'Bishop Bonners bee', so called because of the fiery appearance of the little insect. It is difficult to imagine how a town at that time could have coped with such a disaster. There was no insurance to soften the blow, but no doubt neighbouring towns contributed to some sort of relief fund. Things could have been worse. It was still high summer, the crops were ripening in the fields, there was ample pasture for the livestock and time enough to erect some sort of shelter before the onset of bad weather. Anyway, we can see today the heights to which the human spirit can rise in the face of disaster, and life went on. But even so the poem hints at hardship and despair:

> The Fish and flesh, that I forehande preparde,
> The Drinke, the drugges, the bread, butter and cheese,
> The Hay, the strawe, the wood for whiche I carde,
> All at a clappe, I must forgoe and leese:
> The Catchpole caught them as his lawfull fees,
> Which laide me supperlesse upon my Bed,
> When I scarce fownde a cowch to calme my head.

> The Fruict that late I looued to pare and prune,
> I nowe could reache well roasted from the trees,
> Hunger with care, had harpt so sweete a tune,

> That Bisket Boxes, Carrawayes, and these,
> I leaft at large, for daintie waspes and Bees,
> And now could leape alofte to catch a crust,
> And snap it up with Appetite and lust.

> And doubtlesse, who had heard the Infantes moane,
> For lacke of lodging and accustomed fare,
> Or of the ... and burnt, the grievous groane.

The town at that time probably consisted of one long narrow street from Moorgate to the market with a short branch up the Norwich Road, Church Street, and the Back Street, parallel with the Market Place.

14 Bishop Bonner's cottage.

The lower storey of the houses of that period was half underground and vaulted over; the superstructure being wholly of wood. The poorer sort, of clay, of one storey only, with thatched roof; the floor also clay. The better sort of houses had, perhaps, two or three upper storeys each projecting over the other, in the picturesque manner we see in old engravings. The streets appear to have been lighted by torches, towards the support of which legacies were given in the wills of the 16th century.

So we can picture the Dereham of 1581 huddled beneath the blazing July sun, its thatched, wood-framed houses tinder-dry, waiting for the inevitable spark to start the holocaust.

The town was rebuilt and back to normal by 1597, when Bishop Redman carried out his visitation as if nothing had happened. The records for this show that some fairly trivial matters were investigated; hardly the sort of things worth bothering about in a place just risen from the ashes. For instance:

> Robert Chimney: 'He harboureth in his house diverse persons, whose names they knowe not, some of an incontinent life and others vehemently suspected of the like crime, and that the said Roberte in like manner is suspected.'

Robert Chymbney's name appears in a list of persons who 'had gret losses by the fier and Diverse of them utterly consumed'. He had evidently been able to put his life together again and was enjoying it! Robert Chymney also appears in the muster rolls as a 'selectyd archer' in 1577. In the court books of the Manor of East Dereham of the Queen for 1646 it is recorded that William Neve, Walter Chimney and his wife had assaulted Robert Becket (fined $3/4$d in each case). The Chimneys were never far from hot water.

Another parishioner who incurred the displeasure of Bishop Redman was Arthur Futter (how these old names linger in the parish). His crime was that 'He deteyneth a certaine stocke of the towne without yeilding any accompte'.

Arthur Futter appears to have been a dyed-in-the-wool Elizabethan rascal, for also in 1597 court charges were raised against him that, as a bailiff in the Mitford Hundred, he arrested people without warrant, taking fees before releasing them and, when he did have a warrant for arrest, he refused to take sureties, clapping his victims into East Dereham prison where he charged heavy gaol fees 'whereas never any were paid before'. He sent his under-bailiffs into nearby hundreds to drive men's cattle into Mitford and then compelled the owners to regain them by replevin. He even took bribes from men anxious to avoid jury service at assizes and quarter sessions and gave out that he would exempt anyone who dealt at his mother's shop in Dereham.

15 Arthur, Lord Capel of Hadham (King's army). Beheaded 1648.

The 17th century brought the Civil War, but once again peaceful Dereham was largely passed by. Possibly some parishioners joined an abortive Royalist march on Norwich, for one of the leaders, William Hobart of Holt, was brought to Dereham and executed in the market place. The absentee lord of the manor of Oldhall and Syrricks, the brave and sincere Royalist Baron Capel, took part in the siege of Colchester, was condemned to death and duly lost his head, but not before making history by escaping from the Tower.

Local legend at one time had it that the ruined Wendling Abbey was knocked down by Cromwell's cannon, but it is unlikely he would have wasted any gunpowder on the place which was already in ruins, its fabric being used for road repairs and building. It was possibly in this period that the Puritans visited the church intent on mischief. There still remains evidence of their activities in the broken noses of the figures around the font.

It was the old enemy, fire, once again which caused much grievous damage to the town. It broke out on 3 July 1679, but this time there was no poet handy to record the scene. From the sketchy information available it seems that five people were killed, there was considerable loss of horses and cattle, and 170 houses were burnt down. The damage was estimated at over £19,000.

In 1680-1 East Dereham was included in the list of 'Church Briefs' by which money was raised to assist needy parishes, so at least there was some help forthcoming.

Mention has already been made of the bishop's manor, which by now was known as the manor of East Dereham of the Queen. It is as well, before passing on to the 18th century, to consider the other manors of the parish.

The manor of Oldhall and Syrricks was held by Nicholas Oldhall in 1337, and remained in the family for over a hundred years until 1466, when it passed to the Capel family. A member of this family owned a messuage called Syrricks in Highfield, and the manor became known as Oldhall and Syrricks. The house standing on the corner of Church Street and St Withburga Lane was the manor house.

The manor of East Dereham Rectory was a small manor which included most of the houses on the south side of Church Street and the west side of Baxter's Row. The rectors held the lordship.

Mowles manor during Elizabeth's reign belonged to Thomas Heryng, Gent. It seems to have passed through many hands since the first recorded owner, Adam de Coleburn, in 1257. The manor house stood in a moated site in the Elsing Road, near the parish boundary with Tuddenham. The moat is still there, water filled, within which is an uneven grassy area, dotted with snowdrops and daffodils in spring, just begging for the archaeologist's spade.

16 Country woman wearing pattens, 1640.

Chapter IV

The Parish Chest

As we move into the 18th century, sources of information become more readily available. The church, which has stood for so many years, a symbol of the continuity of parish life, outlasting storm and fire, contains ledger slabs and memorials to local worthies, and the parish chest is a source of much information on the daily life of the time. Dereham actually has a parish chest, and a splendid article it is, though its contents have long since been removed to the Norfolk County Record Office for safe keeping.

An engraved plate on the lid reads:

As a Token of Respect to his Native Place
Samuel Rash Esq.,
On the 1 Day of Jan 1786 Presented to the
Church of East Dereham
THIS CHEST
For the Purpose of keeping together and
Preserving the Deeds, Records and other Writings
belonging to this Parish.
Tradition says this Curious Chest (and Lock) is
upwards of Four Hundred Years Old was taken out
of the Ruins of Buckenham Castle and many Years
since the Property of the Noble Family of the
Howards Dukes of Norfolk and supposed to be used
by them for Depositing their Money and Other Valuables.
Smith Sc Norwich

As for the documents once contained in the chest, a list written on the flyleaf of the Churchwardens' Account book (1701-1773) gives details of the parish papers of the time.

A Schedule of Writings Books and Papers ffound in the Church Chest the 13th August 1753 by Saml Rash and John Ward Churchwardens of the said Parish:

An Overseers Book of Accounts from 1701 to 17... [Indecipherable]

Another Overseers Book of Accounts from 1720 to ... [Indecipherable]

An Old Terrier belonging to East Dereham

1715 A Bundle of papers tied together being Headboroughs Accounts and Bonds given on Acct., of persons being likely to become Chargeable and Examined by Mr. Verdon.

Another Bundle being Churchwardens accts Examined by Mr. Verdon.

1715 A Bundle of old Indres and Recpts

1715 A Bundle of Marriages Births and Burialls and Bundle of poor Rates from 1708 to 1709 and Bundle of Bills and papers relating to Churchwardens accounts

A Bundle of certificates of Marriages

A Bundle of very Antient Writings in a bag belonging to the Church of East Dereham.

Two Bundles of Certificates

Three Bundles of poor Indentures

One Bundle of Bonds of Indemnification of Base Children

One Bundle of orders of Removal

A small bundle of papers Relating to the Session House and new Casting of the Bell

28 Novbr., 1682

A Deed Relating to the Gift of Henry Smith Esq., of £3.4s. to the poor of East Dereham

Reciting a Deed Issued in Chancery 26th July

2 Carl 1st Whereby Lands in great Stoughton in Leicester are charged with the payment to this and Other Parishes

N.B.—A Gift of £8 a year to Thetford in the same manner

8th Septr., 1634

Mrs. Christian Gooch to Mr. Thomas Gooch and the ffeoffmt of an Est in North Elmham in Trust for the said Christian for Life then to Pay £12.10s out of the rents to 36 of the poor of E.Dereham and the poor of sd Parishes then to 20 shyllgs for Sermons then to keep the Houses in Repair and to pay the surplus to the poor.

29th and 30th July 1673

Indres of Lease and Release bet John Pickering of Hoe Thos Moore of E.Dereham Physician of 9 acres of land in Hoe upon condicon as therein Mentioned.

30th Sept. 1675

A Release of Right of Redemption from John Pickering Junr to the said Thomas Moore of the said ?? ines in Hoe.

8th August 1694

Asty Ives Clerk Surviving Trustee to D John Castleton Esq., of ffeoffmts of the Headborough Estate in East Dereham in Trust to pay a leet fee of 13/ 4d and to employ the surplus to such uses as the same have been formerly appropriated for the benefit of the said town.

20th and 21st August 1696

Lease and Release from Mr. Thos Moore Eldest Son of James Moore Bro and heir of Dr.Thos Moore to the Revd. Mr Verdon of Lands in Hoe in Trust for Cloathing poor Widows etc., of East Dereham according to the will of the said Dr Thos. Moore as a Confirmation of his Unkles' Charity.'

17 Wooden panel from St Nicholas' parish chest.

On 11 November, 1852, Parson Armstrong noted in his diary :

Yesterday I looked over our oldest registers in company with Mr Somerby an American Antiquarian and Rev. Mr Grigson, a celebrated archeologian of these parts. The eldest date 1538. Deeds of conveyance of Town Lands go back to 1356.

These documents were valuable—in more ways than one. There is a hint of skulduggery in the vestry from Boston and Puddy's remarks:

Just over a hundred years ago George Carthew, F.S.A., who was a local lawyer and churchwarden, carried out some very valuable research on the history of the town and church. He mentions various documents as being in 'the parish chest' and it is a good thing he quotes from them as they certainly are not there now. What has happened to them we do not know and conjecture is probably libellous. Suffice it to say that one, quoted by Carthew in 'The Town we Live in' was, a year or so back bought by Mr. Gerald Cook from a Manchester dealer.

The documents quoted by Carthew are quite fascinating. To give a few examples from the registers of births, deaths and marriages:

1540—Item the xvij day of June, was buryed Robert Metton, a prysoner.

Item the xxij day of August was buryed Syr Francys Schylyne, prest.

Item the xiiij daye of December, was buryed
Willyam Lavyle als Norman prest.

Item the xiij daye of March was buryed Sr.
John Pers, prest.

[The three priests whose burials are thus entered, were probably parish chaplains, or chaplains to guilds.]

1543—ye xxi day August, was crystenyd mrgarete ye dorter of joone Dokkyng, nec nupta nec virgo.

1546—Item the xvij daye of Maye, was buryed Edmund Atkyns, of the parish clerkys, whyche sunge a goodly basse.

Item the xviij days of June, was buryed Wyllyam Hoo, an old man and a good. I suppose to God.

1547—(last of October christened) Elizabeth ye doutor of Elizabeth Smyth, fiilia populi.

1548—Item the xxiij daye of February, was buryed Sr. John Pykerynge, a prest.

1549—Item the vj daye of Maye, was Arture, the son of Michaell Gurney, borne, and cristened ye sunday nexte aft.

[The presumed author of the Poem upon the subject of the Fire.]

1550—Item the xviij daye of June, was buried Edmund Hawesse, laboryng man. a man above iiij score yeres in age, and as Robart Leke supposed almost v score yeres.

1551—Item the iij day of Apryll, was Rowland Byckerman, a glover and John Browne, taylor, suffred deth charitably for ther offences, and so buryed in thys churchyarde.

[Had this remarkable entry occured two or three years later, we might have supposed these men had suffered for their religion. Perhaps they had been concerned in Kett's rebellion, in 1549.]

Item the xxv daye of July was cristened, George, the sonne of george ledys vycar and the sayde george, was borne on mary magdalens daye before, abowte xj of ye cloke, the dominicall letter then beyng D, whose godfathers were John Browen, the kyngs serjeant, and Willyam Skarlet, of Estderham, and Joan Robarts, my wyffes mother, of the same town, was his godmother; he was borne on the wenisdaye.

[From the particular manner of which Mr Ledys enters the hour of the births of this and other children, he may have been addicted to astrology. He succeeded Roger Balkwell in the vicarage, to which he was appointed by Bonner, 1537, and as another Vicar was presented in 1554, the year after Queen Mary's accession, he either resigned or was deprived of his living. He was not dead, for in 1563, the baptism of a daughter, with the same circumstantiality, is entered in the Register of St Stephen's, Norwich.]

Item ye xxvj day of May, was buryed Roose Kyarter, which departed as she came passyng by the way, wch was borne in Westaker, and was delyueryd of chyld a moonyth befor, at grens hous, as it is thought.

Item the xij day of August, was buried John, the sone of Roose Karter, wch was fatherless and motherless, and founde at ye costes of godly peple in this towen.

Item the xiij day of August, was buryed the chylde of John Bache, named ye creature of God, so named by the mydwyffe, crystened at home, and so departyd.

1552—[31st Oct., was the first that was christened by the Common Book of Prayer, set forth in that year, 'and then wer chrysomes omitted.' Before this there occur entries of crysoms, that is, children still born, being baptised by the midwife before burial. And for many years afterwards, in cases of emergency, infants were baptised by the midwives. The entry of the first burial, according to the service in the Book of Common Prayer, bears the same date, Oct., 31st]

Item the xix daye of November, was christened Olyf, the daughter of a straunger, whose name is not yet knowen, nor her fader: she was borne in the almost hov, (almshouse) at Wydow bells house.

xxvj of Novemb, was buried the child, before christened, of the wydow, a straunger whoise name to me was secretly knowen.

1561—George Tylle } suspensi [hanged] the xxviijth
      George Clerke } day of ye same moneth [March].

1564—Item the xiiij daye of Maye, was cristenyd Willm. the sone of Willm Farwell, of gresnall, and Annes the Dowghter of Wyllm Baxter, of Northall, ys the mother neque uxor neque virgo.

[Some of the entries of irregular offspring are very amusing: the reputed father's name is almost always given.]

1596—Alice Thornley, the daughter of John Thornley, clerk, and Alice, his wife, borne the 24 day of July, betwyst fyve and six of the clock in the morning, being Sunday and Sainct James Eave, and she was baptized the 31 of the same month, being Sunday, in anno do: 1597. The moone being then in the last quarter and in Aries.

[Mr Thornley is even more circumstantial in his entries than was his predecessor, Mr Ledys.]

The Churchwardens' Accounts revealed the rather surprising fact that the 18th-century church carried on a war of attrition against all creatures great and small. In 1728 there are four entries of payments made for killing foxes, at 1s. each, and in 1750:

Paid Jonathan Dutches for a hedgehog, 2d.

Foxes are understandable if they were causing damage but why persecute a harmless and endearing little hedgehog? Perhaps the old country belief that they sucked the milk from resting cows had something to do with it. And, rather surprisingly, jackdaws were also hacked down, despite it being well known that they are the ghosts of departed incumbents of the parish. Evidently the old-timers were no longer welcome.

18 Spare me, I'm only worth tuppence!

It was not unknown to fiddle the books. Parson Armstrong noted in his diary on 18 July 1852:

> In reading the Trustee's Accounts for our Church Fund, I find that considerable sums were at various times expended on 'greasing the buck'. This meant a dinner out of the church funds! Thus under the pretext of repairing a weathercock, these men of the 'good old times' robbed the Church for their own selfish ends.

The 'buck' was the weather-vane placed on the old tower in 1772.

Reprehensible, no doubt, but a meal now and again at the *King's Arms* was small beer compared with the remarkable blow-outs and booze-ups that took place in connection with the 'perambulation' of the parish, or beating the bounds. This old custom, once the Rogationtide practice of blessing the crops, had degenerated into a sort of parish 'knees-up', but it did have a practical use in defining the parochial boundaries.

The Churchwardens Account Books will give some idea of the beer etc., imbibed and the beef etc., consumed by those happy bands of pilgrims taking part in such 'rambleations':

1727— Meat at the perambulation for 103 persons	£1.13. 6.
Spent at George Colpeys	£1.19. 6.
Spent at John Gray's	£1. 1. 0.
At the Haw House	4. 6.
Bread and cakes at Rygreaves	9. 0.

The houses named were probably the places where a halt or station was made. Haw House could have been the present day Haw Hill Farm on the A.47, near the parish boundary with North Tuddenham. It would have provided a resting place for the ramblers plodding out of Badley Moor—and somewhere to broach a barrel.

1753— Wine, Bill for Meat, ale and Punch in going the bounds of the Town, being Entertainment for 80 people, and upwards	£4.15. 0.
For cakes	10. 0.
Half Barrell of mild beer and 1/2 of old at Halfway House	£1. 6. 0.
Spent at Benj. Freeman's	5. 0.
Half barrell of Nogg and half mild beer on Preambulation day of Mr.Ward	£1. 6. 0.
Pd. John Spalding for the common people	7. 6.
Pd a bill at the George for Liquor and eating on the above day.	£3.14. 0.

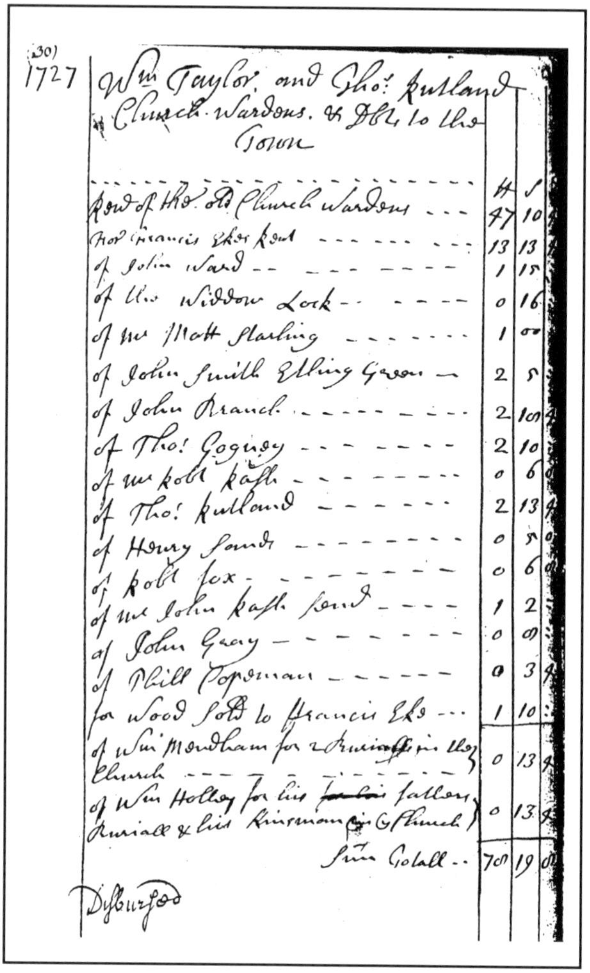

(30)

1727 Wm Taylor and Thos Rutland Church Wardens & Dbts to the Town

	£	s	d
Recd of the old Church Wardens	47	10	
Recd of Francis Ekes Rent	13	13	4
of John Ward	1	15	
of the Widdow Lock	0	16	
of Mr Matt Starling	1	00	
of John Smith Etling Green	2	5	
of John Branch	2	10	4
of Thos Gogney	2	10	
of Mr Robt Rash	0	6	8
of Thos Rutland	2	13	4
of Henry Sands	0	5	0
of Robt Fox	0	6	8
of Mr John Rash Rent	1	2	
of John Gray	0	00	
of Phill Copeman	0	3	4
for Wood Sold to Francis Eke	1	10	
of Wm Mendham for 2 burialls in the Church	0	13	4
of Wm Holley for his fathers buriall & his Kinsman in ye Church	0	13	4
Sum Totall	70	19	00

Disbursed

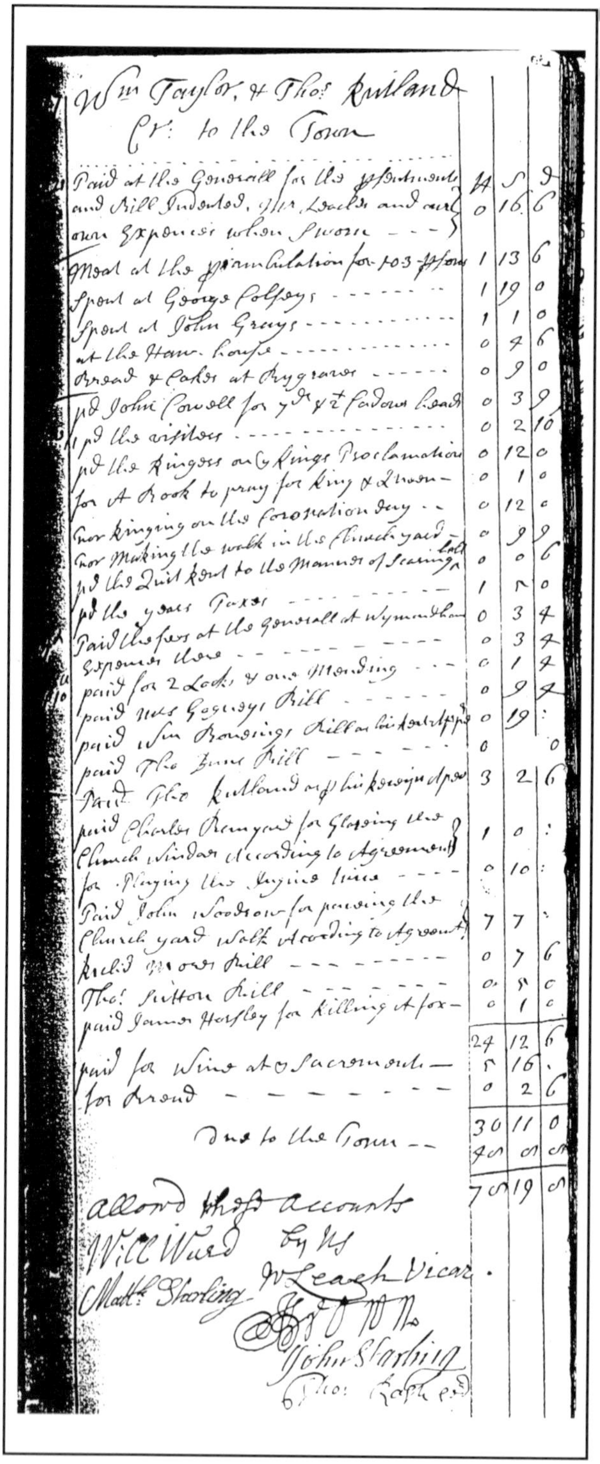

Wm Taylor & Thos Rutland Cr: to the Town

	£	s	d
Paid at the Generall for the presentments and Bill Indented, Mr Leach's and our own Expences when Sworn	0	16	6
Meat at the perambulation for 103 persons	1	13	6
Spent at George Colsey's	1	19	0
Spent at John Grays	1	1	0
at the Town house	0	4	6
Bread & Cakes at Hygraves	0	9	0
pd John Powell for 7 yds & 2 fadom head	0	3	9
pd the visitors	0	2	10
pd the Ringers on ye Kings Proclamation	0	12	0
for A Book to pray for King & Queen	0	1	0
for Ringing on the Coronation day	0	12	0
for Making the walk in the Church yard	0	9	9
pd the Quit Rent to the Mannor of Scarning Late	0	0	6
pd the years Taxes	1	5	0
Paid the fees at the generall at Wymondham	0	3	4
Expences there	0	3	4
paid for 2 Locks & one Mending	0	1	4
paid Mrs Gogney's Bill	0	9	4
paid Wm Bowring's Bill	0	19	:
paid The [illegible] Bill	0		0
Paid Thos Rutland	3	2	6
paid Charles Renyard for Glasing the Church Windows According to Agreement	1	0	:
for Playing the Engine twice	0	10	:
Paid John Woodrow for paveing the Church yard walk According to Agreement	7	7	:
Richd Moor's Bill	0	7	6
Thos Sitton Bill	0	5	0
paid James Horsley for Killing A fox	0	1	0
	24	12	6
paid for Wine at ye Sacrament	5	16	:
for Bread	0	2	6
	30	11	0
Due to the Town	40	00	00
	70	19	00

Allowd these Accounts by us

Will Ward

Matt: Starling

W Leach Vicar

John Starling

Thos Rash

19 Churchwardens' accounts, 1727.

```
1764—  Paid Mr.Potter his bill for
        wine for perambulation          £2. 0. 0.
        Paid Mr.Tooley at the Eagle £2.
        Wm.Bone £2.10.0., Jas.Moore £1.
        their bill for liquor for
        perambulation                   £5.10. 0.
        Paid Mr.Walker and others for
        Cakes for same                  £1.10. 0.
        Paid Mr.Knapp for Beer for do.  £1.10. 0.
```

Samual Rash and John Ward, Churchwardens, do not appear to have been unduly perturbed by such a heavy expenditure on alcoholic refreshment. Perhaps they took the reasonable view that there was no better place for church money to end up than in the pockets of Sam Rash and John Ward, brewers!

In addition to the church accounts, Carthew wrote at length on the Headborough Estate accounts. This was an ancient body, at one time responsible to the Crown for the allegiance of the townsmen, but in course of time had undertaken other duties for the benefit of the community. The following are sample extracts:

10 Febr 1590—monie receyved by me Willm Sheringham sithence I was appoynted to be one of the husbands [stewards] for the hedborrow Lands of Estdereham as followeth vidz

[1] Stewards

Imprimis receyved of Stephen Forman for his half yeare fearme of the Town grove ended att or Lady 1591...............................	xs
Itm rec of Robt Chimney thelder for his half yeare fearme of the closse att Netherds More ended then..................................	xxs

[The rent of the whole appears to have amounted to £4 a year. The account is continued to April 1596.]

Monie to be payd & allowed unto me the seid Willm Sheringham by the Inhabitants of E.Dereham owte the sums of monie before receyved as followeth:

Imprimis I am to be alloed of an account layd owte when I was Constable in pt of the yere 1589 & in pt of the yeare 1590 a appeareth by the accompt	xviijs ijd
Itm layd owte about the placinge of Anthonie Dodds children	xxs ijd
Itm layd owte to Io.Bridges & thother Constables att ye time of there deliv'y of Buttr att Disse for the Queenes household..	xs
Itm payd to Mr Charlton for the Leete fee due att Michelms 1591	xiijs iiijd
Itm payd to the said Constables for the Prisoners at ye Castle	ijs viijd

Itm payd to the sed Constables when they delivd buttr att the place aforesaid for her ma'ties shipps	}	xxijs
Itm payd owte to Mr Futter att his goings to Ester tearme about the dischardgings of the Towneshipp of such Tenthes & subsydie as the Queenes ma'tie dyd gyve towards the repayring of the Towne [after the Fire]......	}	xxs
Itm payd to Willm Crosse for ringinge of the Bell in that winter	}	xs

(2) after the Fire

Itm payd to the seid Io.Bridges & thother Constables when they conveyed 3li to Norwich for the souldiers	}	xliijs iiijd
Itm pd for bread & beare att the accompt when Mr Futter & John Blomefelde were chosen Churchwardens	}	xvijd
Itm layd owte to Crotches wiffe for the kepinge of Cicely Groundson lyinge there of a child...................................	}	xijd
Itm layd out to John Atkinson for dressinge the Towne Armour	}	vs xd
Itm pd to Eldred for skoringe the ij headpeeces	}	xiiijd
Itm pd to Brewster for dressinge them att an other time	}	xijd
Itm layd out to him for wormes & scrues for ye muskitts	}	xijd
Itm fo ij payer of mowldes		ijs
Itm for brasen one of the muskitts		ijs
Itm for horse hire & iij souldiers wages to Wymondam	}	vs
Itm for beare for them there		iijd
Itm for iij souldiers wages & there horse Hire to Denmark	}	vs
Itm to the muster m'r att two severall tymes	}	xs
Itm for xij li of powder		xvjs
Itm for match		ijd
Itm paid to Royse for serving in ye corslett & carryinge the same to Denmark att an other tyme	}	xvd
Itm to Raynolds & Jacobb there		ijs
Itm for beare for them there		iijd
Itm for bringinge home some part of the Armour	}	ijd

Itm for xj li of lead for bulletts	xiiijd
Itm for making them	iijd
Itm pd to Mr Tylnie then for the maymed souldiers for one half yere then ended [Lady 1596] .... }	vjs vjd
Itm layd owte to Michael Lynstead for fetching of a post horse from Thetford .... }	xviijd
Itm to the iij souldiers for two dayes wages when they trayned att Denmark last .. }	vjs
Itm for beare there	vjd
Itm to the Cryer there	vjd
Itm pd to Mr. Ramm for dischargdinge of the townshipp touchinge ye servinge of ye artilllerie besyde the monie I rec'd ... }	vsxd
Itm layd owte att Norw'ch when the souldiers were pressed to go to Flushinge in Holande .... }	xxixs xjd

Md. it is agreed att the accompt made on St.Luke's daye, 1597, that ev'y yeare sereate uppon the seid feaste daye, Churchwardens & husbands for the hedborrowe lands, shall be chosen & the ould shall then yelde there accompts.'

[signed by 13 parishioners.]

1596.

It laid out to Captayne Cottrell muster Mr.	4s 6d
It laid out for a towne peck [pike?]	18d
It for the charge at the last vissitacion	5s 5d

1597.

Pd to the Churchwardens ye firste of maye towards ye Queen's provysion .... }	iiijs

From 'a reconinge for the Hedburrowe growndes from the yeare of our Lord, 1599, to the 4 daye of Maye, in the yeare of Lord, 1602.'

Item layde oute for the makings of the Butts	iijs
Item payd to Mr Ansty for the Kinges Bench & Marshalseaes and maymed souldiers	xxxiijsviijd
'Layd out to Mr Ansty for the Kinges Bench & Marshall seaes prisoners & of the Castle & the muster masters........................ }	xxiijsiiijd
'Item for myne own charges for my horse & my selfe went I to Norwich with the souldiers................................... }	ijs vjd
'Itm payd to Mr Neve for the chargs he was out of aboute the Task (?) for the pke (?) att London...................................... }	xxvs viijd
'Itm payd to Thomas Sheringham wch he had paid to Mr Astye for 1 qr for the prysoners of the Castle............................... }	llljs llljd

Husbands chosen by the Towne, att the Feast of St Mychaell tharchangell, Anno Domini, 1605, John Payne and Thomas Sheringham, for to receyve, take, and paye the Fearme for the headborrowe howse & lands beloninge to Est derham, as follows :

[The receipts for the year, to Michaelmas 1606, were £5 9s. 5d., to Michaelmas 1607, £5 0s. 0d., and to March 1608, £2 7s. 6d.]

A note of such sumes of money as they have layd out and payd for the Towne, synce the time they were chosen Husbans.

Payments

1605—Imprimis pd 3 January for quaterage		xixs vjd
It pd 14 m'che for quaterage..........		xixs vjd
	[This payment occurs every succeeding quarter.]	
1606—It payd 10 May for reparinge the Butts		iijs iiijd
1607—It payd for Iron worke aboute the m'kett bushell......................	}	vjs vjd
It payd for carryinge joyce and plankes} to ston lode bridge....................		xxd
It pd for mendinge the bridge.........		ijs
Now layd out by them wch they were shorte of for money to the ayde for the Towne.................................	}	vijs xd

These accounts throw some light on the methods of keeping law and order in the town:

1630	Payd for mending the hinges of the stocks	vid
1658	For the pillory maken	£6. 1s. 9d.
	For corlen the pillory	7s. 6d.
	For 12 quarts of bere for the rasen of the pillory	1s. 0d.
1659	For the towne well and the wiping post	£1. 6s. 7d.

There was also an entry in 1615 :

Payd to John Mayes for making the Coukestoole	xviis iiid

This was the ducking stool, that excellent little appliance for keeping ladies in order, sadly missed today!

In the accounts also are some intriguing references to bridges :

1655	For laying a bridge at Stonbridge & carrying it doune..............	7s. 8d.
1659	For a bridge maken betwn wivsel and darem (Westfield and Dereham).....	3s 0d.
1702	For getting the bridge up that swam away parting the bounds of Shipdham and Dereham at Toftwood	} amount not given
1761	A payment to W.Earle, R.Alexander. J. Sheringham and Henry Scarlett, Constables, for the repaire of part of St. Toolyes bridge	10s. 4d.

20 Widow Row's geese.

Probably the use of the word 'bridge' is misleading, for these items could hardly have referred to the solid brick structure we know today. They could not have been more than wooden footbridges, as suggested by the one that 'swam away' at Toftwood. Carriages and carts would have had to splash their way through fords. Where St Toolyes bridge was, and why it was thus named, is not known.

Another source of much interesting information was the Manorial Court Book. The following items will serve to show the scope of these courts:

1628   Hugo Browne, gentleman, for permitting branches of trees to overhang the king's way leading from E. Dereham to Mattishall ... fined 3d

Henry Archer, for obstructing the common watercourse in his meadow running from Gallow moor to Stonebridge ... fined 3d

Thos. Scarlett for allowing his sheep on the common pastures of the manor called Moorgate green and Toftwood moor, to the detriment of the lord of this manor ... (fine not recorded)

1631   Simon Chandler and Alice Sherwyn were presentd for receiving into their houses divers persons of suspicious character (fine not recorded)

It was also presented that the widow Row had permitted her geese to be an annoyance before the pit called the Sandpit.

That John Rash had sold bread contrary to the assize fined 5/-

1632   Francis Dey and others, common brewers, were presented for selling ale by unlawful measure and breaking the Assize. Each fined 3d.

1635   A number of millers were presented for the selling of flour in the market by unlawful measure within the precincts of the leete. Each fined 3s.4d.

Ed.Pattrick was presented for selling butter in the market by unlawful pints.

Thos. Vincent was presented for allowing his cattle on Northwoode greene next to the way called Dereham gate.

21 & 22 (Above, right and left) The reredos, St Nicholas' church.

23 (Left) The bailiff being molested.

1638   Ann Perrymond was presented for not maintaining her well in Wake's lane in sufficient repair

1641   Several persons were presented for molesting the Bailiff, John Neve, gentleman, whilst he was fishing the ponds of Etling Green, and violently carrying away the fish.

Chapter V

Tales of Arcady

In the 18th century we have visual aids for our researches into the past. Because of the two fires, Dereham (excepting Bishop Bonner's cottage) has no graceful, picturesque old Tudor buildings that are the glory of so many old market towns. Instead, most of the older buildings are solid, prosperous looking Georgian houses, and we can see how well-to-do 18th-century gentlemen lived when we look at Hill House, for instance. But in this century we must step outside the parish bounds to get the full picture, for by this time Dereham had become the focal point for a wide area of Mid-Norfolk.

This was the 'Arcady' which Dr Jessopp, rector of Scarning and Head of the Norwich School, often referred to in his writings: 'A prosperous and fertile area, bounded roughly by the upper waters of the Wensum and Yare and watered also by little trout streams like the Blackwater, Tud and Penny Spot'.

Armstrong gives a mouth-watering description of this green and spacious land:

> October 16th 1852—'Drove to Houghton Hall. The road all the way was an instance of that 'still life' which is remarkable to those who have lived in or near London. There were endless fields in a high state of cultivation, but the question always interposed, who labours in them? For mile after mile is traversed without seeing a human being'.

It is hard to imagine such a scene these days: it is hard also to realise what an intense stillness must have prevailed, for we are told (Armstrong again) that when the guns of Landguard Fort carried out their firing practice the local pheasants would crow, and that an explosion at the Hounslow powder mill on 10 April 1859 was plainly heard in Dereham.

In this gracious land there lived in comfortable, almost idyllic circumstances noble lords in their halls, well-to-do gentlemen in their opulent manor houses, and plump clergy in their roomy parsonages. Most of them had connections with Dereham in one way or another.

There was, for instance, Sir Edward Astley of Melton Hall who presented the town with its obelisk, built on the site of the Sandpit, where in the previous century poor Widow Row's geese had annoyed the townspeople, and which one is inclined to liken to Hardy's description of Castorbridge:

> The old play-house, the old bull-stake, the old cockpit, the pool wherein nameless infants had been used to disappear ...

In 1881 the old Sandpit was opened up in connection with the sewage work then going on, and, as somebody feelingly commented in the margin of *The History of Dereham* held in the Norwich Local Studies library—'It stank!'.

Canon Macnaughton-Jones described the presentation of the obelisk in his booklet, *East Dereham—its Historical and Archaeological Features*:

24 The obelisk.

In the year 1757 Dereham was reputed to be the dirtiest town in the County, A subscription was raised towards re-paving the town, to which Sir Robert Walpole, the celebrated Premier, contributed. The spot where the obelisk stands was a pit of filthy water. This was filled in, and Sir Edward Astley, the then Member of Parliament, presented the town with the obelisk. So pleased was Walpole with the improvement, that he gave a public entertainment to the inhabitants at his seat at Houghton. Forgetting their host's Whig proclivities, under the influence of his good wines they burst into the Jacobite song and chorus—'All Joy to Great Caesar'. However, Walpole sent them home happy in him and themselves.

During the Second World War the obelisk was removed and, it is said, thrown down a well; pity somebody does not pull it out again and put it back where it belongs.

The building which did much to enhance the town's popularity with the neighbouring gentry was undoubtedly the Assembly Rooms. It was built in 1756 at a cost of £400 and made use of the materials of the old Market Cross which had stood on this site. A picture of King George III presented to the

25 The dirtiest town in the country.

town by Viscount Townshend in 1766, hangs in the main room today; a fine imposing and regal portrait it is, suitable for the pomp and circumstance associated with the building. In the days when a coach journey to London was considered too perilous to be undertaken for pleasure, the Assembly Rooms was an attempt to create a local substitute for the gay London society. We can get an idea of the scene at such a place from *Pickwick Papers* when the misadventures of the unfortunate Mr Winkle in Rochester are described, but there is no reason to suppose that there ever was a 'pistols for two, coffee for one' confrontation on the Neatherd at dawn!

Assemblies continued to be held long after the coming of the railway made the London journey much easier. Parson Armstrong recorded the scene in 1861:

> December 12th—We took our darling Helen to the Assembly, her first Ball. The darling looked to be so charming in her parent's eyes. She enjoyed herself beyond her expectation and danced 14 of the 20 dances marked for the evening. There were 120 present—all the best families in the neighbourhood whom we knew, and many of the aristocracy visiting in those houses whom we did not know. Lord Sondes made himself as affable and his lady as imperious and exclusive as ever. As for the toilettes, they were of every imaginable hue and kind.

The building, of course, was used for purposes other than Assemblies. This notice appeared in the *Norfolk Chronicle* on 6 January 1838:

Lord Sondes Birth-day.

The Conservatives of East Dereham and the Neighbourhood intend to dine together at the Assembly Rooms, East Dereham on Monday the 22nd day of January to celebrate the birth-day of the Rt.Hon. Lord Sondes

Col. Mason in the chair.

Dinner at 5 o'clock precisely.

Tickets 10/6d each to be had on application to Mr Howard, King's Arms, Dereham.

And from the *Norfolk Chronicle* 5 May 1838:

The Anniversary of the Birth-day of the consistent and truly patriotic Nobleman
The Right Honourable the Earl of Leicester
Will be celebrated at the Assembly Rooms, East Dereham on Monday 7th May 1838,
Brampton Gurdon Esq., President.
Mr William Beck, Vice-President.
Dinner at four o'clock.

Tickets 9/- each may be had at the Eagle Inn, East Dereham

Of the aforementioned gentlemen, Lord Sondes lived at Elmham Hall, Col. Mason at Necton Hall, Brampton Gurdon at Letton Hall, Viscount Townshend at Raynham, and, of course, the Earl of Leicester at Holkham.

Not all the occasions at the Assembly Rooms were formal and upper-crust. The building was also used for popular entertainment, as an interesting replica of an old poster in the *George* shows:

Assembly Rooms, East Dereham.
Positively for 2 nights only
Mr Jacobs
The celebrated Illusionist, Ventriloquist and
Improvisatore.
Having just concluded a course of Entertainments at
Ipswich, Yarmouth and Norwich where was attended by
numerous and highly respectable audiences, and whose
performances in other places have been honoured with
the presence of the following distinguished
Personages:-
Her Royal Highness the Princess Augusta
The Lord Chancellor
Rt Rev the Bishop of Rochester
His Grace the Duke of Wellington
His Grace the Duke of Richmond
His Grace the Duke of St Albans
Her grace the Duchess of Marlborough
etc., etc., etc.
Begs respectfully to inform the Nobility, Gentry and
Inhabitants of East Dereham and its vicinity that he
proposes giving
Two Entertainments at the above Room
On Wednesday and Thursday evenings 11th and 12th
December, 1833, When he hopes to be honoured with
that support which it will be his most conscious
desire to merit.

The entertainment was in three parts; Tricks and Deceptions (which appeared to be a conjuring display), Ventriloquism, and—

Mr Jacobs will conclude his performances with an extemporary song and poetize on any subject given him by the Audience after the manner of the Italian Improvisatori.

Admission prices were

Front seats 2/-, Back seats 1/- (children half-price in front seats only).

Mr Jacobs seems to have risen in his profession for in 1844 he had achieved the billing of 'Wizard of Wizards' at the Theatre Royal, Norwich.

Entertainments such as this, of course would be another factor in attracting people from the surrounding parishes. Theatrical performances, for instance, were given from time to time, from about 1749, by a company from the Theatre Royal, Norwich, probably in a barn behind the *King's Head*. It was at one of these performances that Cornishman Thomas Borrow, serving in the West Norfolk Militia, was bewitched by a local girl, Anne Perfrement, playing in the 18th century equivalent of the chorus line, and married her in 1793. In 1803 a son, George Henry Borrow was born, who was to bring fame to the town by his writings. Anne is described as 'a strikingly handsome girl with black flashing eyes and an olive skin, oval face and black hair'. Thomas was a stocky 5 ft. 7½ ins. That he should sire a son 6 ft. 3 ins. tall and swarthy just shows that the ways of Nature are indeed wonderful. The suggestion, expressed by some romantic souls, that George's natural father was a tall dark stranger who forsook his gypsy campfire on Badley Moor for the warmth of Mrs Borrow's bed, as the opportunity arose, should be discounted!

The Norwich Company were later replaced by the Norfolk and Suffolk Company of Comedians, under their renowned manager David Fisher, who built our theatre in 1815.

Such occasions, whenever possible, would have been timed to coincide with the full moon period, to make travelling after dark easier. This reliance on the 'Parish Lantern' was slow to die away, and it is said that the frugal folk of North Walsham would for many years turn out their gas lamps in the streets on moonlit nights.

Another popular entertainment was the travelling circus. Some idea of the programmes offered can be gleaned from this advertisement, which appeared in the *Norfolk Chronicle* on 6 January 1821:

Pantheon Olympic Circus.

J. Cooke

begs to inform the public in general that he intends opening a circus at East Dereham on Tuesday 9th inst., in Mr Harvey's Timber Yard for a short time previous to his going to Lynn Mart where he will have the honour of exhibiting his wonderful Troop and beautiful stud of Hanovarion and Arabian Horses whose docility and management excel any other Troop in the world.
Ladies and Gentlemen taught the polite Art of Riding and Management of their Horses on Road and Field.
Good fires kept in the circus to render it comfortable.
The Doors will open at Six o'clock each evening and the Performance commences at Seven o'clock.

Norfolk Chronicle, 20 January—A further Olympic Circus advert:

Change of Performance
Mr Cooke will introduce his grand Trampoline when he will throw Somersets through small Hoops 3ft in diameter, likewise over a number of horses, and lastly will throw his wonderful Somerset thro' six balloons—The beautiful cream coloured Hanovarian Horse Wellington will dance correctly to the tune of Nancy Dawson on a small table!

And then, of course, there was sport. Probably the most popular sport at that time was hunting, and a brief mention is made in Norfolk Annals of a meeting held at the *King's Arms* in 1830 to consider the establishment of a pack of hounds. The outcome was not reported, but Dereham Races were held in 1857 under the patronage of the Norfolk Hunt; and the Rev. B.J. Armstrong, who had been a keen rider to hounds in his youth mentions several instances of meeting the hunt in the neighbourhood. In one instance he put aside clerical decorum and joined in the chase, remarking afterwards 'It fare to do me good'. There was evidently plenty of opportunity locally for those wishing to partake in this traditional sport. Race meetings on the other hand were surprisingly infrequent, in contrast to some other Norfolk towns where they were held annually.

There was, however, a solidly established tradition of cricket in the town, in fact, the County Ground was at one time in Dereham, on the Hoe Road. In addition there was the Dereham Club's own ground on Norwich

26 The Hunt Meet outside the *King's Head Hotel, c.1908.*

Road, where the leisured gentlemen of the time passed peaceful days occupied in this pleasant and civilised pastime.

From the *Norfolk Chronicle*, 31 August 1822:

On Monday and Tuesday last a match of cricket was played at Dereham between the Gentlemen of the Dereham and Swaffham clubs, which after a fine display of science by both, was decided in favour of the latter—

	Swaffham	Dereham
1st innings	64	31
2nd innings	101	82

Decidedly less civilised or pleasant was the entertainment offered in Mattishall in 1825:

A main of cocks will be fought at Mattishall near the Swan Inn on Monday 20th June between the Gentlemen of Norwich and the Gentlemen of Mattishall; a double days play, 13 mains and 6 byes for £10 a battle, and £25 the odd.

Feeders—Stafford, Norwich

Overton, Mattishall.

A good ordinary.

A pair of cocks on the pit at 12 o'clock.

Other 'entertainments' to be found in the county at this time included bare-knuckle pugilism, bull-baiting and camping (a decidedly rugged variant of football), played by 'men' after the Gentlemen had put away thair bats for the season.

From the *Norfolk Chronicle*, 22 September 1832:

Norwich Cricket Ground.

The lovers of camping are respectfully informed that a MATCH for TEN SOVS will be played by Twenty Men, on Tuesday the ninth of October. It will take place on the Norwich Cricket Ground, and commence at Three o'clock precisely.

Arrangements have been made that cannot fail to ensure good sport.

Refreshments of all sorts to be had on the Ground.

27 Quebec Castle.

Although the Assemblies and various other functions attracted the most prominent members of society in the locality to Dereham, the town itself could boast of no comparable high-ranking family.

We never had a resident lord of the manor until Armstrong referred to W.W. Lee-Warner of Quebec Hall as 'our local squire and magistrate'. Quebec Hall, or Quebec Castle as it was once known, was built in 1759 by our local beer baron, Sam Rash, appropriately enough, it is said, on the site of one of his pubs. After his death other tenants tried their luck and sometimes bankrupted themselves in keeping it up. It was not until the Lee-Warners moved in that it acquired a touch of gentility. Actually the family name was Bagge, but Dr Bagge had married a Miss Lee-Warner and some of his children preferred to go through life as a Lee-Warner rather than a Bagge (especially the ladies).

28 (Left) Face on the wall of Hill House.

29 (Right) Hill House.

The other house of class in the town is Hill House, once the home of Sir John Fenn, the antiquarian who published the Paston Letters. He died in 1794. His widow, Lady Eleanor Fenn, who did much good work in the town, is described by George Borrow in *Lavengro*:

> Pretty, quiet D—, thou pattern of an English town—with thy one half-aristocratic mansion, where resided thy Lady Bountiful—she, the generous and kind, who loved to visit the sick, leaning on her gold-headed cane, whilst the sleek old footman walked at a respectful distance behind

During the 18th century professional men were establishing themselves in the town. Attorneys, surgeons, apothecaries, auctioneers and bankers. Tradesmen, brewers, builders and good quality shops all added to the attraction of the town and a modest prosperity was founded which continued to grow without check.

In 1777 the 'Paupers Palace' was built at Gressenhall—more trade for the town. Stage coaches were operating services from the principal inns and the Turnpike was opened.

Towards the end of the century the shadow of the Napoleonic War spread over the country. The threat of invasion was very real and the Norfolk coastline was especially vulnerable.

> He who would old England win,
> Must at Weybourne Hope begin.

runs the old couplet; the water at Weybourne was deep very close inshore, and ideal for landing troops. Sure enough it was near Weybourne that an incident occcured which was recounted by Charles Loftus in his book, *My Youth by Sea and Land*. Charles was the son of Dereham-born William Loftus (we shall mention him later), who was living at Stiffkey at the time.

> Upon one occasion when my father and mother were in London, it was reported that the French had landed at a place called Weybourne, about six miles from our house. One of the principal tenants came up to the house to tell us that we had better have the horses harnessed and the carriage ready in case it should be necessary to start. Great was the excitement of the maids and the old housekeeper, who at once began to pack up our clothes and their own in the carriage trunks. The housekeeper stowed many things away in secret places where she thought those French thieves, as she called them, would not find them.

> The farmers also were very busy harnessing the horses, ready to put them into the waggons to convey the poor people of the village out of reach of the enemy, should they advance. The yokels who had been trained every Sunday afternoon to the use of the musket and bayonet were mustered on the church green.

> In the midst of all this excitement the noise of drums and fifes were heard coming down the Wells Road. We children ran to the beach wall which looked over into the road, 'Lawk-a-mercy' cried old Sally, the head nurse, 'What shall we do?' The old coachman ran out with his whip to see what was the matter. A horseman dashed past us up the road, crying out 'They are coming' at which announcement there was a general shriek among the maids, 'Don't be such fules, you maids—they are the volunteers from Wells a-coming to fight the French!' And sure enough they were. At their head rode Parson Tickel upon a Rozinante, very similar to that on which Don Quixote is described to have ridden when he set out upon his adventures. The drums and fifes kept playing to the lively tune of 'The girls we left behind us' while the men went on with a quick and steady march.

This is a specimen of many similar scenes that occurred in various parts of the country, for the dread of the threatened French invasion was universal. It turned out, however, to be a false alarm.

Further inland, but just as ready to defend their country, were the men of Dereham, who formed two troops of Yeoman Cavalry; no doubt the fox-hunting fraternity of the neighbourhood were prominent in their ranks—eager to chase the 'Frogs' for a change. They made their contribution to the defence of the Norfolk coastline as this excerpt from the *Norfolk Chronicle* of 7 January 1804 shows:

> Yesterday se'nnight the 2nd troop of East Dereham Loyal Cavalry, commanded by Capt. Crisp left Yarmouth and arrived at Dereham Saturday afternoon having performed their regular routine of garrison duty at the former place ... On their arrival they were congratulated by a vast concourse of people amidst the ringing of bells ... The officers and a great part of the Troop dined together at the King's Arms.

In the ranks of the other troop was one Sergeant Thomas Munnings, who featured in an episode that would have delighted dear old Stanley Holloway. Fortunately we know about it because Thomas was as ready with a pen as with a sword, the following are extracts from his book *Munning's Fancy*:

> To Captain Wodehouse, March 7th, 1797.
>
> Dear Sir,
>
> After what happend yesterday, I should esteem myself inattentive to the credit of our troop and regardless of my own honour, if I hesitated to make an immediate appeal to you.
>
> The foul mouth of Mr Clements has at last been opened against me, in a manner the most abusive and the most unprovoked.
>
> I will briefly state it to you:-
>
> Having discussed and agreed to some 'Rules and Regulations' with as little difficulty as could have been expected; and having appointed (as by your direction) Mr Crafer, our quarter master, and Messers Mays, Kirbell and Palmer, our sergeants: I was proceeding (by the express desire of Lieutenant Hyde) to PLACE the troop; that every MAN knowing his situation, and the horses acquiring a familiarity, our FUTURE operations might be rendered the EASIER to us. I had completed the 'FRONT RANK'; when, going up to him, I said "Mr Clements, will you be so OBILIGING as to take the Centre of the Rear? He answered, "I shan't take no place but what I have got; I'ont run the hazard of my neck, nor endanger my life for you, nor no man: let Mr Hyde take the Centre if he will and be d—d. for I shant take it; and what's more I 'ont come no more' after to day' nor nobody SHANT make me neither!

The outcome was inevitable.

> On March 15 1797; At a special meeting of the members of the troop of Norfolk Yeomanry Cavalry, commanded by Captain Wodehouse, it was RESOLVED by a committee of the whole troop, that the Behaviour and Language of William Clements, a private in the said troop, was mutinous and subversive of the ORDER and DISCIPLINE which ought at all times to prevail amongst SOLDIERS; and unanimously agreed, that Lieutenant Hyde be requested, in the name of the troop, to transmit an account of their RESOLUTION to Captain Wodehouse, and to desire that he would forthwith discharge the said William Clements from the said troop, and call upon him 'to deliver up his arms, accoutrements and cloathing'.

In gratitude, perhaps, for having rid them of such an unruly member, the troop presented Thomas with a medal. The event is recorded in the *Norwich Mercury*, 5 June 1797:

> The 4th troop of Norfolk Yeomanry Cavalry presented the Rev. T.C. Munnings, an emblematical medal bearing the Medallion of the King,

(which the artist has represented by a Guinea) surrounded by symbols of 'Religion, Liberty and Law' which was the motto; on one side of the medal the standard of the troop, with its motto ' Our God, our King and our Country' and on the reverse, expressing a compliment to Mr Munnings, this motto 'Be England prosperous and the World in Peace'.

From drilling his troop, Thomas turned to drilling turnips—they did not answer back. He modestly wrote:

I am animated with a fond belief that Posterity will regard me as an experimental agriculturist, whose earnest aim it was 'To scatter Plenty o'er a smiling land'; to introduce such beneficial innovations as might render England—the exhaustless granary of the world.

He intended to attain this noble aim with his patent turnip drill, which he describes in loving detail:

My DRILL then consists of a tin box (about 8" long and 5" diameter in the middle) in the shape of a barrel, affixed to the axis of a wheel about 22" high, vertical with the same, and, in its evolutions dropping the seed through small apertures in the middle of the barrel, which middle is, by means of a screw, variably distant from the wheel from 12 to 14 inches. With this extremely simple and very cheap machine, (the price about one guinea) I began my work by having the tops of my ridges set out with the common Norfolk two-horse plough; and when the same plough takes up the furrow next to the top, it is immediatly followed by the Drill, which drops the seeds upon the first mould the instant it is turned up. The person driving the Drill (which work may be done by a boy or woman) is then followed closely by a one-horse plough, the overshot mould of which as quickly buries the seed, which is thus deposited in regular and very straight lines or rows, at equal distances of about 18" apart. After it is thus sown, the land is harrowed or rolled in the same direction in which it was ploughed, and the consequence is, that my crop grows as regularly in rows as a gardener can plant cabbages.

One can understand Thomas's concern about turnips since, as rector of East Bilney, he would benefit from the turnip-tithe, an important source of clerical income in those days. He was assiduous in collecting his tithes as can be seen from this notice in the *Norfolk Chronicle*:

Notice is hereby given that I,

Thomas Crowe Munnings

Will hold my Composite Audit at my House at Gorgate on Monday, the Fifth day of November 1832.

That I shall be ready to begin Business at Nine o'clock in the Morning of that Day. That I expect and desire all who have payments to make will settle them (in full) before One o'clock at which hour (at the Public House in Beetley known by the sign of the Punch Bowl) a plentiful Dinner, of 'Plum Pudding and Roast Beef' will be ready. And that Ten Bottles of Spirits will be sent for the purpose of making Punch, in order to facilitate and promote Digestion.

What with his Volunteers, his turnips and his tithes, it is a wonder that Thomas ever found time to marry or to bury any of the good folk of East Bilney!

He did, however, find time to dabble in verse:

Like 'Hearts of Oak' to bear the brunt,
The Norfolk Volunteer,
To all his foes will 'show his front'
But never show his rear!

The Rev Mr Munnings was not the only clerical 'character' in the neighbourhood in those delightful days. There was the Rector of Gressenhall for instance, described by Armstrong:

> Mr Hill of Gressenhall—one of the old school who are nearly extinct. He plays cricket with the village lads on Sunday evenings, cuts off his own meat at the butchers—imbibes any quantity of port, and service over, descends from the pulpit, opens his pew door, offers his arm to his wife, and marches out of the Church before any of the congregation think of moving.

Then there was Mr Tacey of Swanton:

> Taken from the stocking looms by some benevolent individual and sent to Cambridge. He became tutor to Mr Lombe, owner of the Bylaugh estates, who presented him with the living worth £1000 a year. Bishop Stanley made him a rural dean.

Armstrong must have written this somewhat wistfully, for his own stipend was probably less than half that, and the bishop certainly never made him a rural dean.

The parish of Scarning harboured two fine characters. One is described by Dr Jessopp:

> The Rev John Beevor, a big burly, sloppy sort of man. They tell how he had an enormous appetite and could never get enough to eat at home. There was, and still is, a second-rate inn at the adjoining town of Dereham, where some of the coaches used to change horses and the carriers put up their vans. Here a good deal of eating and drinking went on. The people say that when the parson had devoured all he could find at the rectory—and in those days people used rarely to dine later than four—he would be driven down to the 'George', and as one of my old people put it 'there Parson Beevor'd George hisself—leastwise that was what I've heard them say!'

And the other? Old Jessopp himself, no less. He was a character to stand comparison with the best or to use the word he himself favoured, an 'Individual'.

He was remembered with affection by H.W. Saunders, author of *A History of the Norwich Grammar School*:

> Jessopp, like Marley's ghost, carried his own atmosphere about with him, and no place was the same after his entry. There were many reasons for this. First, his very form and looks made one realize that it might be true that man was made after God's own image and I never tired looking at him, whether poring over a book, stalking his study and reciting Tennyson or some other thing which pleased him, denouncing or praising this and that, or walking through Scarning as pastor and sometimes as archaeologist.— Yes, he mesmerised one.

However, he failed to mesmerise Parson Armstrong when they met at Gressenhall. Here is Armstrong's version:

> September 2nd 1880.
> Went to the reopening of Gressenhall Church. There was choral service by the village choir who had evidently been well drilled, and who got through it without a mistake. Many Dereham people were there. Dr Jessopp preached one of his eccentric sermons without any reference to the object which had brought us together. Sitting in the sedilia, I could hear very little but I caught the words 'Mumbo jumbo'—'to stave in the beer barrel and send round the teapot is no cure for our faults'—'the flashy young Jew of our Lord's day with his penny paper'—'dynamite has power to blow this church into a million atoms,' which last—as we had been commemorating its rebuilding—I thought inopportune.

30 The Reverend Augustus Jessopp DD

Jessopp died in 1914 aged 91, in joyous anticipation of the next world, about which he had definite, if somewhat unorthodox, ideas:

> I often think that one of the joys of the life hereafter will consist in being permitted to project oneself at will into remote periods in the past and to hold converse with primeval man at one time, or with Roman or Saxon or Dane at another and for a while to take part in the life of bygone ages. What a curious joy it would be, for instance, to hob-a-nob for a season with the pigmies of the Meiocene, listening to the clicks of human creatures like unto 'barnacles or apes' with pendulous breasts and 'foreheads, villanous low' and watch them capering multitudunous round some Mastodon in difficulties or tickling a Deinotherium with a fishbone arrow.

We also had our own homespun Hornblower in the person of Arthur Lee-Warner, R.N. He went to sea in 1804, at the incredibly early age of 11, and served in the East and West Indies. He took command of HMS *Esk* in 1821, and remained with her until 1823 when she was paid off, leaving him 'on the beach' on half pay. As readers of naval stories will know, it was necessary to have the backing of a rich and influential patron to make progress in the Service; and so we find him, in 1827, seeking the help of Lord Bentinck:

> To Rt. Hon Lord W. Bentinck,
> 59, Lower Grosvenor Street, London.
>
> My Lord,
> I have been nearly three and twenty years in the Navy and my most assiduous wish has been to rise in the service. I am perfectly aware how impossible it is to obtain promotion without employment. I am therefore most anxious and willing to serve in any ship or on any station it may please the Lords of the Admiralty to command with the promise of ultimate promotion but I really do not wish for employment during peace without the prospect of rising in the Service. I have thus my Lord taken the liberty of stating my wishes to your Lordship (?) I shall ever feel most grateful for the (?) of interest you are about to exert whether I am fortunate enough to get my promotion or not. I have the honour to be Lord your humble servant
>
> Arthur Lee-Warner.

He died in 1842 and is commemorated by a ledger slab in the church which shows his rank to have been 'Commander, R.N.'.

The ledger slabs in the church are a useful source of information about local people living before directories were printed. There is one, for instance, inscribed: 'Peter Stoughton (Gent) died May 11th 1805'. Parson Armstrong had a story to tell about this gentleman:

> July 26th, 1877
> Travelled back to Dereham with a Mr Stoughton of Bawdeswell Hall. He told me of a certain Peter Stoughton, who had lived in Dereham, and who made it his custom to go into the church at 10pm for private prayers. Leaving his lighted candle at the West end, he went to the altar for that purpose. He was terribly alarmed one night by seeing a light gradually advance up the church to where he was. It turned out to be a rat, which had made prize of the candle and was carrying it in its mouth still alight. The rat dropped it on seeing the man and left him in the dark.

Another slab which brings to mind a story is that of Mr J.S.W. Daniel of Dillington Hall:

31 In pursuit of pigs.

32 The Reverend B.J. Armstrong.

Norfolk Chronicle—4th September, 1819.

Early on Sunday morning 2 pigs were stolen from the farmyard of J.S.W. Daniel Esq., at Dillington, near Dereham. Mr D., hearing a noise got up and observed a man put the pigs into a cart standing in the road with which he drove off. He immediatly pursued him and overtook him at Mattishall where a scuffle ensued and the thief who proves to be a notorious character, made his escape, leaving the cart containing the pigs in the possession of Mr D. He was apprehended the next morning with 2 of his accomplices.

A fine picture Mr D must have made, galloping through the darkness, nightshirt flapping, in hot pursuit of his pigs!

The town of Dereham is not given to self-advertisement; even the tiniest toot, however muted, blown on its own trumpet, would be considered awfully bad form, and so some of its most worthy sons are almost unknown even in their birthplace. The parish register contains the entry:

1752—Baptised Feb.7—William, son of Captain Henry Loftus and Diana his wife.

Henry Loftus, like Thomas Borrow, was a soldier, stationed at Dereham on recruiting service. William followed his father into the army, distinguished himself in the American War and became a General Officer and Lieutenant of the Tower of London. He was Member of Parliament for Yarmouth. We have already mentioned his son Charles, whose book describes so vividly the hardihood and adventurous spirit of Englishmen of those days.

In 1766, fourteen years after the birth of William Loftus, another William was born in Dereham—William Hyde Wollaston, son of Francis Wollaston, vicar of Dereham. He had a somewhat varied career, first becoming a doctor, then, when he was passed over for a hospital appointment, abandoning medicine for science. He was outstandingly successful, made a fortune, and became president of the Royal Society.

We also had an artist—Edward Barwell, who in 1861 had two paintings accepted by the Royal Academy. One of these sold for £180. Constable's masterpiece, 'The Lock', sold earlier in the century for £150. Today it is valued at many millions. Search your attics, dear readers: if you've a Barwell up there gathering dust, you may be a multi-millionaire!

And of course there was the Rev. B.J. Armstrong, whose remarkable diaries, if published in full, would rank with the best in the land.

So it was that the town itself needed newcomers to recognise, and to publicise, its quiet beauty.

A visitor staying at the *King's Arms* in the late 19th century wrote of the view from his bedroom window down Church Street:

33 Stoneroad Bridge.

> The red-tiled uneven roofs of these ancient dwellings, with the sun glinting upon them, contrasted powerfully with the solemn grey of the grand church tower close by. Church, tower and cottages compound a charming picture, as full of colour and as delightful to look upon, as though the scene were designed by an artist.

Parson Armstrong had not been in Dereham very long before he fell under its spell and, on 14 July 1852, recorded an experience which surely must rank with any 'impulse from a vernal wood', experienced by Wordsworth in Lakeland.

> Sometimes great happiness vouchsafed to us without any proximate cause and without being able to assign any specific reason why it should be felt so powerfully at a particular time. This evening during my ride the sun set in perfect splendour behind the dark woods, before me was a surface of waving corn just turning towards ripeness, the cottagers were enjoying themselves in their trim gardens, at this season so gay with flowers, in the distance was Dereham town on the hill slope and the evening bells were ringing. I reined in to repeat Keble's exquisite evening hymn.

(Possibly Hymn No. 25 in *Hymns Ancient and Modern* 'Sun of my Soul, Thou Saviour Dear'.)

Unfortunately the pleasant environment of past years is dwindling under today's harsh mechanical conditions on farms and roads. Who would think, for instance, that Stoneroad Bridge, on the Dereham to Mattishall road, now surrounded with a chicken factory, a scrap car yard and a sewage farm, was once a spot so pleasant that children would walk all the way from Etling Green to paddle in the stream and to catch minnows and millers'-thumbs. In the quiet of the evening sweethearts would, undisturbed by any passing traffic, carve their initials on the parapets of the bridge.

Chapter VI

Sixty Glorious Years—and More

The late Kenneth Clark, in his TV series 'Civilisation' said:

> There have been times in the history of man when the earth seems suddenly
> to have grown warmer or more radio-active ... . I don't put that forward as
> a scientific proposition but the fact remains that three or four times in
> history man has made a leap forward that would have been unthinkable
> under ordinary evolutionary conditions.

He was speaking of an earlier age but it is surely applicable to the 19th
century, when an outburst of energy and enterprise changed old, slow, bu-
colic England almost beyond recognition. The century began with Nelson's
wooden walls, the plodding carrier's cart and the romantic stage coach. It
ended with the electric light, the telephone and the motor car.

For Dereham, the first news worthy event of the century was recorded
in the *Norfolk Chronicle* of 3 May 1800:

> Yesterday se'nnight died at East Dereham in
> this county of Norfolk the celebrated poet
> William Cowper, Esq., of the Inner Temple,
> author of 'The Task' and many other beautiful
> productions. This amiable and very interesting
> character was born at Gt. Berkhampstead in
> Hertfordshire November 15th 1731. His father,
> the Rector of that parish was John Cowper
> DD, nephew to the Lord High Chancellor
> Cowper, and his mother was Ann, daughter
> of Roger Donne, Gent., late of Ludham Hall
> in this county.

This was followed three years later by the
birth of George Borrow. As he wrote in the opening sentence of *Lavengro*:

> On an evening of July, in the year 18-, at East
> D-, a beautiful little town in a certain district
> of East Anglia, I first saw the light.

Borrow and Cowper are the two famous
names associated with Dereham, though neither
spent much time here. Cowper was a sick man
when he came to stay with Mrs Mary Unwin at a
house in the market place where the Cowper Congregational Church now stands. He wrote only one
work during this period, the grim poem *The Cast-
away*. When Mrs Unwin died, to avoid upsetting
the ailing Cowper, she was secretly buried at midnight in the parish church. When Cowper died he
too was buried in the same way. Parson Armstrong
recorded that in 1879 he buried a Mr Cooper, aged

34 Cowper Memorial Window.

35 (Above) William Cowper aged 60 years.

36 (Left) Cowper Church, Market Place.

91, who could recall Cowper's midnight funeral—Dereham men have long memories (except when they owe you money!).

George Borrow, our famous 19th-century super-tramp, did not spend much time in these parts either. In *Lavengro* he wrote:

> I have been a wanderer the greater part of my life; indeed I remember only two periods, and these by no means lengthy, when I was, strictly speaking, stationary. I was a soldier's son, and as the means of my father were by no means sufficient to support two establishments, his family invariably attended him wherever he went, so that from my infancy I was accustomed to travelling and wandering, and looked upon a monthly change of scene and residence as a matter of course.

The first national census was taken in 1801 and gave the population of Dereham as 2,505. On 22 October that same year a Ball and Illuminations took place to celebrate the Peace of Amiens (a very short-lived peace, called by its opponents 'The Peace that passeth all understanding'). Anyway, it was a cause for celebration and the event was recorded by Parson Woodforde:

> 22nd October 1801. Dereham Ball this Evening and Illuminations on Account of Peace with other Rejoicings. Mrs Custance and Daughters are said to be there as were also, Lord and Lady Baynham and Daughters.
>
> Cold NW. wind and some rain.

To round off the year the new Dereham Workhouse was opened and 117 paupers moved in from Gressenhall Union. This stood in Norwich road; the site is still called Union Square.

In 1806 the Rev. George Thomas died—the last of our vicars to wear a three-cornered hat and cauliflower wig. He was remembered for catechising the boys under the pulpit, teaching them prayers at Christmas, and, as presents, gave each a pair of shoes and stockings. He was the vicar who solemnised the marriage of Thomas Borrow and Ann Perfrement on 11 February 1793.

The Rev. Charles Hyde Wollaston followed him and served us for 44 years; during this time he must have seen many changes, not all to his liking as the next chapter will show. Wollaston maintained the old 'High Church' tradition at Dereham, as the youthful George Borrow remembered in *Lavengro*:

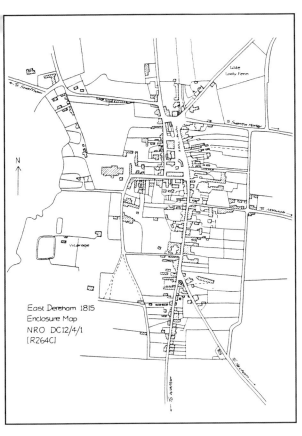

East Dereham 1815
Enclosure Map
NRO DC12/4/1
[R264C]

37 Map of Enclosure, 1815.

I was regularly taken to the church, where from the corner of the large spacious pew, lined with black leather, I would fix my eyes on the dignified high-church rector, and the dignified high-church clerk, and watch the movement of their lips, from which, as they read their respective portions of the venerable liturgy, would roll many a portentous word descriptive of the wonderous works of the Most High.

As a matter of interest, it was Wollaston who got rid of those old box pews. He also built the present vicarage, for in those days the clergy housed themselves, often in considerable style, as many of the lovely old parsonages scattered throughout the country bear witness.

In 1811 the next decennial census was taken: the town had 1,276 males and 1,612 females, 551 inhabited houses and 16 standing empty. It is worth mentioning that, in that year, 'a beautiful comet observed in the north-west, the tail of immense length (from 12 to 14 degrees) and the whole brilliant beyond description'.

In 1814 an event took place which must have lingered long in the memories of local people. It was described in the *Norfolk Chronicle* of Saturday 16 July:

Thursday se'nnight the return of peace was celebrated —. The morning was ushered in with a merry peal and firing of guns. Immediately after Divine Service a grand procession took place with the effigies of John Bull and Bonaparte which were afterwards placed on top of the shambles. At 2 o'clock 1800 poor inhabitants sat down in the Market-place to a most excellent dinner of plum pudding and beef, which was conducted with the greatest regularity—At five the signal was given to proceed to Neatherd Moor where the sports immediately commenced which afforded considerable diversion to upward of 6000 spectators among whom were an elegant assemblage of the beauty and fashion of the town and neighbourhood whose animating smiles, combined with the fitness of the weather to render the scene truly gratifying. The evening concluded with a bonfire and a grand display of fireworks in the Market-place.

But the war was not yet over, Waterloo was still to come; it was not till 1815 that the Forty Years Peace, lasting to the Crimea, began. A remarkable era of change and progress dawned, and for Dereham the first great change happened that very year with the publication of the Parliamentary Enclosure Award, which gave permission for most of the extensive commons of the parish—over 840 acres—to be cultivated. The enclosure of common land was an emotive issue, and had been since Kett's Rebellion of 1549. Somebody wrote rather bitterly:

Tis bad enough in man or woman,
To steal a goose from off a common,
But surely he's without excuse,
Who steals the common from the goose.

EAST DEREHAM

INCLOSURE.

To *The Reverend John Nelson*

We, whose Names are hereunto subscribed, being the Commissioners named and appointed in and by an Act of Parliament passed in the fifty-second year of the reign of his Majesty King George the Third, entitled " An Act for Inclosing Lands in the Parish of East Dereham, in the County of Norfolk," do hereby give you Notice, that we have by our Award, in writing, bearing even date herewith, and signed, sealed, and delivered by us, pursuant to the directions of the said Act, and of an Act of Parliament passed in the forty-first year of the reign of his said Majesty, and entitled An Act for Consolidating in one Act certain provisions usually inserted in Acts of Inclosure, and for facilitating the mode of proving the several facts usually required on the passing of such Acts ". allotted unto you.

One piece of land in East Dereham aforesaid containing One Rood and Thirty five Perches bounded by Norwich Road towards the North by land by your said Award allotted

---

East Dereham Inclosure 1812

Commissioners' allotment to the Revd. John Nelson

One piece of land in East Dereham. 1 rood and 35 perches bounded by
Norwich road to North
      Land allotted to Bartholomew Fisher to East
      Rev. Nelson's own land to South
      Eighthly described private road to West
Fences to be made and kept in good repair against public and private roads and against
Bartholomew Fisher's land.

The Commissioners have studied and agreed the ancient copyhold and leasehold messguages
buildings and lands and tenements in the Parish of East Dereham, viz:—

Copyhold Lands and Tenements of the Rev. John Nelson held of the Manor of East
Dearham of the Queen

One piece of land in East Dereham marked No.127 on the Inclosure plan containing 1-2-
0, where a stable and outbuildings stand, occupied by George Cooper, bounded by
      Land of Elizabeth Girling to North
      A Lane called Back Lane to East
      Land of William Howard in part of South
      Land of Thomas Amis in rest of South
      Land of Job Margetts }
        and Thomas Amis } respectively in part of West
      Rev. John Nelson's own land in rest of West

Another piece of Land in East Dereham marked No.128 containing 11-0-37 acres bounded
by
      An ancient Lane to North
      Land of Harriott, Dowager Countess of Essex to East
      Another ancient Lane in part to South and to West

Another piece of Land in East Dereham marked No.129 containing 2-0-6 acres bounded by

Land of John and Reuben Eastoe to North and East
An ancient Lane to South
Land of the King's most excellent Majesty to West
Land of Jane Buck to South
Neatherd's Moor to West

Another piece of Land in East Dereham marked No.207 containing 3-2-35 acres bounded by

Turnpike Road from East Dereham to Norwich in part to North
Land awarded in exchange
to Rev. Charles Hyde Wollaston to rest of North and in part to East
Land of Thomas Wright to rest of East and to South
Land of Robert Watts to West

Another piece of Land in East Dereham marked No.208 containing 5-1-2 acres bounded by

the Turnpike Road in part to North
Land of Robert Watts to rest of North and in part to East
Land of Harriot Dowager Countess of Essex to rest of East
Road from East Dereham to Mattishall to South West

Another piece of Land in East Dereham marked No.209 containing 9-3-28 acres bounded by

Same Turnpike Road to South
Rev. John Nelson's own land to East, North and West

Another piece of Land in East Dereham in 3 Inclosures marked No.130, containing 23-1-0 acres

An ancient Lane to North
Land of Harriot Dowager Countess of Essex in part of East
Rev. Nelson's own land to rest of East and to South in part
Turnpike Road East Dereham to Norwich to reat of South
Lands of John Eastoe ⎫
Reuben Eastoe ⎬ respectively to West
William Lane Robinson ⎭

<u>Land Copyhold of the Manor of Old Hall and Syrricks in East Dereham together with Yaxham</u>

One piece of Land in East Dereham marked No.205 containing 1-1-18 acres bounded by
Award Land of Rev. John Nelson ⎫
        and Bartholomew Fisher ⎬ to North
Land of Robert Watts to East
Land of Thomas Wright to South
Cherry Lane to South West

Another piece of Land in East Dereham marked No.206 containing 1-2-37 acres bounded by

Land of Robert Watts to North and East
Turnpike Road East Dereham to Norwich to South East

<u>Awarded in exchange for Land allotted to the Revd. Charles Hyde Wollaston</u> (see plot 207 above)

One piece of Land in East Dereham containing 3 roods lying in an Inclosure of Land of Rev. Nelson's own called Grove Close.

All exchanges have been agreed and signed.

<u>Rights of Common on Elting Green</u>
are allocated to the people named below as owners of Estates in East Dereham which had Rights of Common over the Commons and Waste Grounds in East Dereham and which are most conveniently situated for Commonage upon that tract of land.
There shall exist for ever hereafter Sixteen Rights of Common over Elting Green each entitling the owner or proprietor to feed and depasture on Cow Heifer Mare or Gelding from 12 o'clock noon on 10th May every year until 1st March next following.

Nevertheless, the demand for grain, arising from the war, was so imperative that age-old common rights were ruthlessly extinguished, though in most cases the former commoners were compensated by the grant of small allotments of land. But even so, it must have seemed an enormous upheaval in a way of life that had been going on for centuries.

With increased grain production came the demand for better transport and distribution. One solution was a 'navigation'. The proposal, put forward at a meeting in the Assembly Rooms in 1819, was to make the Wensum navigable and link it to Dereham by a canal. Unfortunately the opposition of influential land-owners along the route stifled this idea at birth and the vision of a maritime Dereham was consigned to that sad land of 'What-might-have-been'.

39 Quebec Street.

With more grain to deal with, increased milling capacity was necessary and by 1836 a new tower windmill was built in Cherry Lane, equipped with the latest technology as the sale notice in the *Norfolk Chronicle* described:

> That newly erected and substantially built TOWER WINDMILL eligibly situated within ten minutes walk of the Market Place of East Dereham comprising five floors and driving two pairs of stones, with capability of adding a third pair, with patent sails, winding herself, iron shaft, flour mill, jumper, sack tackling and all other necessary machinery on the latest and most improved principles, with stable and cart lodge and about one acre and three quarters of excellent Freehold land adjoining.

There had been mills in Dereham for hundreds of years, but something entirely novel was being built at the same time up Windmill Lane (now Quebec Road). It was the gas works, and with its completion in 1835 the first step towards our modern technological society was taken. It was sold to a company of 16 proprietors in 1840 and by 1845 there were 50 public gas lamps lighting the town.

Mechanical ingenuity was not confined to the town. Out on the farms threshing machines, powered by circumambulating horses were coming into use, replacing the flail-threshers. These redundant men suffered hardship and hunger and reacted with violence and arson—the so-called 'Captain Swing' riots. Ugly scenes took place throughout the county but the parish of Dereham escaped, thanks to the soothing influence exerted by a troop of the 1st Royal Dragoons stationed here. When things quietened down, to show our gratitude, the privates and NCOs were given a dinner at the Assembly Rooms (1 January 1831). An incident of this period worth recalling took place when Crow Hall, Downham Market was besieged by one such mob. The owner's daughter, Miss Dering, bravely slipped through the besiegers' ranks disguised as a gypsy, to fetch help. She later became Mrs Bulwer of Quebec Hall. Arising from this incident 16 people were sentenced to death, but only two were hanged.

Before we consider the next and undoubtedly the most important of the 19th-century innovations, the railways, let us take a look at the last years of old, unhurried rural Dereham. There were still stage-coaches rattling cheerfully in and out of the coaching inns, and carriers' carts plodding out to various destinations. The turnpike road from Norwich to Swaffham was maintained by the tolls collected at the Etling Green and Scarning gates, and roads generally were kept in good enough condition to enable the Norfolk Regulator coach to depart from the *Eagle* at 6.45 a.m. and arrive in London at 7 p.m. This inn was also the starting point of the Self Defence to Norwich

40 Elvin's Coachworks.

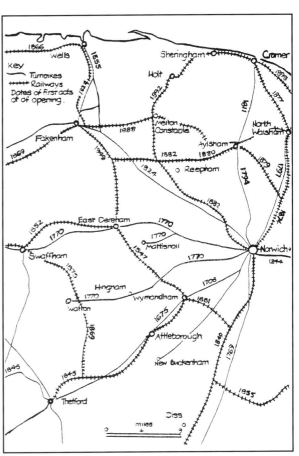

41 (Above, top) A scene at the tollhouse at Etling Green.

42 (Above) Stage coach.

43 (Right) Map of turnpikes and railways, Central Norfolk.

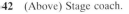

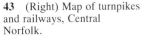

44 Cherry Lane Mill.

every Monday at 9 a.m. and Wednesday and Saturday at 8 a.m. The *King's Arms* (which stood in the market place, on the site of Woolworths) had the Mail to Lynn, Birmingham, etc., at 9 a.m. The Day Coach to Lynn 6 p.m. and to Norwich at 11.15 a.m. was shared between the *King's Arms* and the *Eagle* alternatively. In addition there was the Union to Lynn at 11.15 a.m. and to Norwich at 7.15 p.m. On Saturdays the Earl of Leicester would pass through at 8 a.m. on its way from Beetley to Norwich and return at 6 p.m.

Stage coaches, thanks to Christmas card artists, are everybody's idea of Olde England, especially with plenty of snow lying around, but that other vital part of early 19th-century road transport, the carrier's cart is less well known. There were several serving Dereham and it was here that the smaller inns got a look-in. For example, the *King's Head* had Hacon and Ball's vans to London on Mondays and Thursdays at 6 p.m. Green and Archer's van left the *Green Man* (a vanished inn that stood in the High Street) for London also on Mondays and Thursdays. From the *Chequers* (which stood at the bottom of Swaffham Hill) John Allen went to Swaffham and Norwich on Tuesdays and Fridays. Wells and Fakenham were served by Wm. Raven from the *Lord Nelson* (this stood where Nelson Place now is) on Friday mornings. The same inn was the departure point for Thos. Towler, who went to Heacham and Norwich on Fridays. There were others, some leaving from private addresses. It would be very interesting to know more about this early form of road haulage. The *George* is not mentioned in these schedules,

45   Waterloo House, Canterbury House, Mount Pleasant and *The George*, c.1908.

probably because it specialised in the hiring of post chaises to those who could afford them. Chaise and coach travel was expensive, but people with little money and plenty of time could travel on the carriers' carts. It could not have been very comfortable perched on miscellaneous freight, including livestock, that the carriers picked up on their travels. It was not fast, either; for example, travellers from Saxmundham to London were said to write home from Melton, the first over-night stop, to let their loved ones know that all was going well on their journey. This was a distance of about 12 miles! The conveyance was a hooded wagon pulled by six horses and controlled by a man with a long whip riding alongside on a pony.

It seems opportune at this point to mention briefly a business which had been established to meet the demands of this horse-powered age— Elvins, the coach and harness makers. The business was founded in 1818 in Norwich Street premises, now the Memorial Hall. They built landaus, broughams, victorias, dogcarts, cars, phaetons, wagonettes, farmers and tradesmen's carts, all of which were, it was claimed, specially noted for elegance of design, soundness, light running and superior finish. Their harnesses and saddles were also of high quality. It has been said that a carriage for the Czar of Russia was built here, though just how he became connected with our town is not clear. C.N. Elvin, who took over the business from his father, was an expert on heraldry, and a prolific writer on the subject. His works included *Book of Mottoes, Anecdotes of Heraldry, Synopsis of Heraldry, Dictionary of Heraldry* and *Handbook of the Orders of Chivalry, War Medals, Crosses with their Clasps and Ribbons.* He also painted the 12 shields in the north aisle of the church. He built Eckling Grange, where he died in 1894, after which the business seems to have declined.

The early 19th-century newspapers often carried sale notices of farms, private houses and inns. A glance at one or two examples will prove interesting because they show how the prosperous farmers and gentry lived, and the trade carried on at the inns.

Watering Farm, East Dereham.
By William Chambers
On Monday and Tuesday, the 1st and 2nd days
of October. 1832.

All the valuable farming-stock, implements in Husbandry, Dairy and Brewing utensils, and part of the Household Furniture of Mr John Clements, at the Watering, East Dereham, in the county of Norfolk; comprising a capital cart stallion, five years old, three superior horses and mares, two two-year old cart colts, one three-year old do., two foals and two capital ponies, dairy of ten fine milch cows, one year old bull, three year old heifers, capital road waggon, two harvest ditto, two load tumbrils, two three-quarters ditto, two patent wheel ploughs, two gangs of harrows, two pairs of ditto, two hand rolls, with shafts, team and cart harness, plough ditto, and a set of gig ditto, bullock straw bins, and a variety of farming implements.

Dairy and Brewing Utensils, and Household Furniture—four double milk leads, barrel churn, butter keeler and measures, cream pots and two pails, brewing copper, mash tub, under-beck, four beer vessels and other tubs, mahogany tables, wainscot ditto, dressing ditto, small chest of drawers, two feather beds, chairs, three stump bedsteads, mahogany bureau ditto, and other useful articles.

The sale to begin each day at Eleven o'clock precisely.

The Farming-stock carriages and implements the first day - Dairy, brewing utensils, and household Furniture the last day.

Refreshments will be provided for the company.

46   Market Place with the *King's Arms*.

47 The *Eagle Hotel*, complete with brass eagle, 1915.

Or, if you fancied a town house, this desirable residence was available:

East Dereham, Norfolk.
To be let.

With immediate possession

a very convenient and comfortable house, in good repair, situate in the most pleasant part of East Dereham, fit for the reception of a respectable Family (now the residence of Mr Collison); consisting of an entrance-hall, nearly 18ft square, laid with Portland stone, parlour, study and housekeepers room, good kitchen and suitable offices, beer cellar and wine vaults, five bed chambers and five attics, wash-house, capital brew-house, laundry etc.

The outbuildings consist of a double coach-house, stables, stabling for seven horses, harness house (with fire-place) cows house, coal-house, wood-house, shoe house, knife house etc., are all new and of the first description, and the Garden (part of which is walled in) contains with the Shrubbery and a large oval Fish-pond therein 1A. 3R. 12P.

For further particulars apply (if by letter post-paid) to Messrs E & G Cooper, Solicitors, East Dereham, 13th October, 1832.

It was not unusual to keep cows in towns in those days. Parson Armstrong, serving on the local board of health, commented on the 'fearful nuisances' he found at the back of some of the houses in 1853, remarking that attempts at pig and cow keeping in a town must always be 'injurious', and he noted 19 cases to be reported to the Board of Guardians.

In 1838 the *Eagle* changed hands: the new landlord advertising himself as follows:

Eagle Family and Commercial Inn
East Dereham, Norfolk.
William Cooper.

Begs to inform the Nobility, Gentry and Public that he has taken the above inn and trust by assiduity and attention, to merit a portion of their favours. Commercial Gentlemen may confidently rely upon their comforts being personally attended to. Wines and Spirits of the finest quality.

Commercial gentlemen, or mercantile travellers, or bagmen, as they were variously called, were moving around in quite large numbers even in those days. William Cobbett referred to them as 'bumpers' because they travelled in gigs instead of on horseback and incurred his displeasure by monopolising the best rooms at the inns. No doubt they found good customers here, such as the enterprising Mr Bond, for instance, who advertised:

A real friend to the Pocket
T.M.Bond, East Dereham,

> Finding his system of ready money, small profit and Superior Articles give so much satisfaction, he is determined to make it more extensively known a saving of 20 to 30 percent is obtained on purchasing the following articles at this establishment, which are all quite new - Stout prints 4d yard, best London do 8d to 11d yard; calicos, sheetings, hosiery and drapery of every description at reduced prices. In the silk room will be found an Elegant Assortment of the newest and most fashionable colours in French and British Du Capes, Laventines, Gros de Naples, Sarsnetts, etc., a choice collection of much admired figured Orleans Dresses, printed muslins, French and British shawls, scarfs. handkerchiefs etc. Bonnet and Cap ribbons, Urlings, Brussels and thread lace, veils and squares, kid gloves, hosiery, etc, etc,. A quantity of the fashionable and much-admired Thibet Shawls from 15/- to 30/- usually sold from 25/- to 50/- .

Mr Bond was evidently running the 1831 equivalent of today's discount store.

Advertisements for patent medicines were frequent in the early 19th-century newspapers. Unscrupulous quacks would sell you a cure for anything. Here are one or two examples:

> Barker of Dereham sells anti-impetegines at £1.13.0. per bottle also Whiteheads essence of mustard (a certain remedy for chilblains) at 2s 9d per bottle.

Anti-impetegines were a not so certain remedy for the 'social disease', or rather were used to offset the side effects of mercury taken as a treatment for that disease. As the old saying goes: 'One night with Venus, a lifetime with mercury!'. Barkers also stocked:

> Dr Steers opodeldoc—cures rheumatism, spasms, burns, scalds, cuts and stings.

As readers of the *Ingoldsby Legends* will know this was a potent linament in the right hands! (see *The Black Mousquetaire*, Canto II).

Or, if you were really poorly, you went to Dawson of Dereham and bought his Life Pills, at 1s. 1½d. and 4s. 6d. per box. They worked like magic: 'By increasing the energy of the brain, and pouring new life and vigour into the constitution they enable nature to make incredible efforts for the expulsion of disease, before organic destruction'.

In 1809 a new fire engine was purchased and it was decided to charge £2. 2s. 0d. for its hire. In 1817 it was put to good use, as reported in the *Norfolk Chronicle* of 16 August of that year:

> On Sunday last, about 4 o'clock in the afternoon, a fire broke out in the dwelling house of Mr Mann, farmer, of Scarning, which entirely consumed the same, but by the timely arrival of the engines from Dereham it was prevented from extending to the out-buildings and stack-yard . Great credit is due to a number of persons from Dereham, for their alacrity upon the occasion, amongst whom were several gentlemen whose judicious directions were of essential service.

There was no fire brigade in those days. If your house caught fire you had to hire the engine and man it yourself—lets hope you had alacrious neighbours!

There was not much in the way of local government to organise services such as fire-fighting. The 'Vestry' served as the local authority and its members were the local property-owning parishioners. To keep the law they appointed a parish constable, who was given a decorated truncheon as a symbol of authority and told to get on with it. Presumably it was thought that this was enough to over-awe any malefactor—but it was not, and by the end of the 18th century the system had almost broken down. Horse-stealing, in particular, was rampant and newspaper notices such as the following were all too frequent:

Fifteen Pounds reward.

Stolen

From a stable belonging to Mr Samuel Bates of East Dereham, in the night of Tuesday, the 14th instant, or early the following morning. A bony black horse of the Hackney kind, in good condition, six years old, about 15 hands high, roman nose, ears long and thin, the ends turning inwards ... A saddle and bridle in the Stables were also stolen at the same time. Whoever will give such information as will lead to the conviction of the offenders, may receive a reward of TEN POUNDS from the said Samuel Bates and the further sum of FIVE POUNDS from the fund of the East Dereham Town Association by applying to

G Johnson, Treasurer,

East Dereham. June 15th, 1825.

In the absence of a police force the East Dereham Town Association had been formed to combat crime. Its members paid a subscription and in return were assisted in tracing the culprits by the display of notices such as the above and the offer of a reward. In 1840 the County Police were formed with John Abbot as Superintendent of the Dereham Division. An old photograph, taken in 1891, shows an establishment of 17 men.

Also badly in need of overhaul and rationalisation at that time was the education system. In 1840 the situation was improved by the opening of two new schools, the British and Infants in London Road and the National at the bottom of Theatre Street. Before this there had been a plethora of small privately-run schools that advertised themselves with newspaper notices such as:

Mr Buck's Academy

Will open again on Friday, January 19th 1821. Terms for Board and Education.

Under 12 years of age—20 guineas per annum, above that age 24 guineas. Parlour boarders 30 guineas per annum. Entrance 1 guinea. Latin, French and drawing, half a guinea per quarter each.

East Dereham Seminary for young Ladies.

The Misses Wigg respectfully announce that the recess will close on Monday January 24th 1842. The system of education adopted has been attended with the most gratifying success, and includes English, Grammar, Composition, Writing, Arithmetic, Geography, History and Plain and ornamental Needlework.

Terms for boarders.

Under 10 years of age 18 guineas per annum. Above 10 years of age 20 guineas per annum. The situation is most salubrious, and a large garden is appropriated for the Recreation of the Young Ladies, the domestic arrangements impart the comforts of Home; and the strictest attention is paid to the health and mental improvement, as well as to the moral and religious principles and habits of their pupils.

48 East Dereham Secondary School for Girls, now Neatherd High School.

All very fine if you were well-to-do, but there was no chance of working-class families finding that sort of money. It is rather difficult to ascertain the educational facilities available to the poor in the early years of the century. There were three Sunday schools by 1785 thanks in part to the efforts of our 'Lady Bountiful', Dame Eleanor Fenn of Hill House. In these, '80 persons are brought up with the knowledge of their duty to God and man' according to a contemporary newspaper report. Sunday schools in those days taught reading and writing in addition to giving religious instruction, and were a valuable means of keeping children out of mischief on Sundays.

In 1811 the 'National Society for promoting the Education of the Poor in the Principles of the Established Church' was formed. It appears that this quickly led to the building of a further school in Dereham. A tombstone in the churchyard commemorates the death of Theodore Stoakley, master of the National School for 22 years. He collapsed and died in 1834 at the school 'in the midst of his pupils and in the presence of the Vicar'. So there was at least one school provided for the education of street urchins.

An 1836 directory listed 10 'academies', five of which took boarders. Dereham had no Grammer School, comparable with say, Hamond's School in Swaffham, but in the next parish, Scarning, stood William Seckar's Free School, a very good establishment which sent many scholars to Cambridge University. Some of its Old Boys rose to high positions in the land. Dereham gentlemen like Mr Barry Girling of Humbletoft, for example, were educated there.

And so we reach the railway age, which brought to an end a way of life reaching back several centuries. The Dereham of, say, 1840 would have been perfectly recognisable to someone living in 1740, but it would have appeared a very unfamiliar place to someone in 1940. The first railway reached here in 1846, when the Norfolk Railway linked Wymondham to Dereham with a single line track, opened for freight traffic in December of that year, and for passengers the following February. The line was built by the celebrated railway engineer, Samuel Morton Peto; the project went smoothly and even the railway navvies, who had acquired a well deserved reputation for hell-raising, were complimented on their good behaviour. The

49 Sidings and the Maltings, pre-1921.

railway opened a door through which the first trickles of the 20th century soon began to seep. In 1848 the East Anglian Railway's King's Lynn—Dereham line finally reached Dereham, having been proceeding from Lynn by fits and starts since 1846. By this time the Eastern Counties Railway had taken over the Norfolk Railway and were asking an annual payment of £500 for E.A.R. to use the station. This the latter thought exorbitant and built their own station at Lynn Hill. In 1849 the line from Dereham to Fakenham opened, later to be extended to Wells. Thus Dereham became an important Mid-Norfolk railway junction, a bustling busy station much larger than one would expect to find in a quiet country town.

Among those enjoying the convivial parties held to celebrate the opening of the railway in 1846 was a Mr Gidney (in his case a dinner for 80 gentlemen at the *King's Arms*). He was vice-chairman for the evening in recognition of his work in seeing the bill through the House of Lords committees. He was a typically energetic Victorian entrepreneur and quickly put the railway to good use by exhibiting his wares at the Great Exhibition of 1851. On stand 556 he displayed models of his 'improved wire fence' and portable iron sheepfold (the hurdles so familiar at one time on the local farms). The railways had made the Great Exhibition possible by transporting the materials for the Crystal Palace, the exhibits and of course the visitors.

Mr Gidney's business prospered, and his handiwork can be found scattered far and wide across the county. In 1862 a new door was built into the south wall of the chancel of the parish church. It was a close copy of the original medieval door, even down to the ornamental iron scroll-work, except that, on the new door, this is embossed with the name 'Gidney'. Mr Gidney was not a man to waste a good design, and soon this pattern of ornamental ironwork spread like a rash through Dereham. It can be found

50 Ironwork door.

sprawling all over the doors of the Cowper church, it decorates the doors of his own St Nicholas Ironworks in Cowper Road, and even reached as far out as the doors of the twin mortuary chapels in the Cemetery. Mr Gidney had evidently insinuated himself into ecclesiastical circles, for as far apart as North Creake and Ditchingham can be found grilles for the underfloor heating of the churches made by 'Gidney'. He also made many of the stout iron railings still to be found round some of the old better-class houses—up Quebec Road, for instance. For some reason the business faded towards the end of the century, no Gidneys are to be found in 20th-century directories.

Undoubtedly, the railways gave a great fillip to local trade and industry. At last the farmers had their much-desired transport for grain, livestock and fertilizers. Huge maltings, the largest building by far in the town at that time, arose alongside the railway. Two industries not connected with agriculture were established; Skipper's leather factory, near the station, by 1874, wàs employing 100 men and Brown's boot and shoe factory in Church Street had 50 employees. Steam power was coming more and more into use, and here the railways assisted by bringing coal much more cheaply than by the long, slow road journeys from the nearest ports. Coal was also used increasingly for domestic purposes, as other fuel supplies dwindled. By 1864 four coal merchants were listed, including the ubiquitous Mr Gidney, ever ready to seize the main chance.

In 1850 a very important passenger stepped down onto the platform of Dereham station. He was the Rev. B.J. Armstrong, come to take over the vicarage after the death of the Rev. C.H. Wollaston. He was a devoted diarist, and his volumes have fortunately been preserved. They give a picture of life in 19th-century Dereham seen through the clear, kindly eyes of someone who obviously enjoyed every day spent in this old place, although he was a Londoner and must have found conditions here very different. He made full use of the railway, even if it was the notorious Eastern Counties, butt of many a complaint and jibe in the contemporary newspapers. On 15 May 1853 he wrote:

> Whit-Monday. Came up to London with my wife and children in an excursion train. It consisted of nearly 40 carriages and vast crowds availed themselves of the privilege.

In pre-railway days people only travelled out of grim necessity; now they did it for pleasure. They made 'excursions' and special trains were laid on for this purpose. Armstrong returned to Dereham on 19 May:

> I started by the 8 a.m. train and by 3 p.m. was carrying on the routine of Parochial work just as if it had never been interrupted. It is only with such practical examples that we understand what wonderful things Railways are and how time and space are annihilated by them.

But the wheels did not always turn so smoothly:

December 17th 1853—

> Returned to Dereham by the 5 o'clock express and left Fothergill at Ely. About 7 miles further the wheel of the tender broke, threw the carriage off the line and dragged it along, ploughing up the earth at a fearful rate. It then came to a standstill and we all got out. Providentially no accidents happened and we were near Mildenhall station where we waited 2 hours while the carriage was righted and the Telegraph set in motion. Arrived home at 11 instead of 8.30.

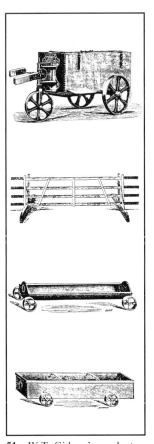

51 W.T. Gidney's products.

52 Dereham railway station, *c*.1910.

This suggests that the normal time of a journey from London to Dereham was a quite remarkable 3½ hours. On another occasion he had an even more hair-raising experience:

> October 12th 1880. On our way to Buxton our engine-driver shunted on to the other rails to attach another carriage, when the express came to meet us on the same line of rail. With admirable presence of mind he changed the points and the express passed us safely by. Deo Gracias.

The Armstrong diaries are invaluable when studying life in mid-19th-century Dereham. His clear fuss-free style brings events to life as if they happened only yesterday. We can see behind the august doors of the Assembly—we can peep into the mansions of the local nabobs and we can meet a fine selection of his parishioners, both rich and poor.

The population in 1851 was 4,385, an increase of over 500 in 10 years. In 1852 occurred the death of W.W. Lee-Warner of Quebec Hall, 'our local magistrate and squire' as Armstrong called him, adding 'he took little or no interest in parochial affairs'. However, his memorial in the church recalls 'his noble, generous nature ever keenly alive to the wants of his fellow creatures whom he relieved with no sparing hand'.

On 14 September of that year the town witnessed the colourful spectacle of a troupe of horse-riders, bands of music, a man driving a ten-in-hand and a carriage drawn by an ostrich.

The Mechanics' Institute and Library was opened in 1853. Parson Armstrong had been prominent in getting this established and he wrote: 'let us hope that many may be saved from vice and dissoluteness by means of our forthcoming Institution'. He went to London and from 'Brown's Immense Book Store' selected volumes suitable for perusal by apprentices and artisans. They included a beautiful Shakespeare, 10 large volumes of Biography, three of Brands Popular Antiquities, two of Schegel's philosophical works, five of the Spirit of British Essayists, History of British India, Lectures to a Mechanics' Institute and some others. The inaugural lecture took place on 9 November; Lord Sondes of Elmham Hall, the Institute's president with his daughters, the Misses Milles, were present to hear the Rev Bath Power of Norwich lecture on 'Physical Science and its relation to the Arts and conveniences of Life'. Mr Power gave an interesting exhibition of the Electric Telegraph, after which Parson Armstrong gave a 20-minute speech. Then, presumably, the artisans and apprentices could settle down to their light reading, thus avoiding any inclination towards vice and dissoluteness!

There was much activity in the town around this time and Armstrong was behind most of the proposals for change and improvement. He commented, on 21 November 1853:

> Attended as Trustee a meeting of the Headborough to take into considertaion the feasibility of erecting a Corn Exchange in substitution of our present Shambles. If we can get something architectually good this would be the finishing stroke to what all the 'bagmen' say is one of the prettiest towns in England.

On 1 December he triumphantly recorded:

> At a Vestry it was unanimously resolved to pull down the Shambles which now disfigures our otherwise handsome market place. It is an eyesore with which I was much struck on first seeing Dereham but hardly hoped to get the nuisance removed with so little trouble.

The Shambles was a cluster of butchers' stalls standing in the market place.

Another eyesore which displeased him was the mock-Gothic Bath House, erected in the previous century over St Withburga's Well. This too was duly demolished in 1855 and replaced by the present garden. And so the Bath House came down and in 1857 the Corn Hall went up, but not without bitter controversy. Just what all the fuss was about is not clear—probably vested interests were involved. Its opponents claimed it was built on a public highway over Lion Hill. The dispute reached the Court of Chancery which ruled that the Hall should remain because of its benefit to the community.

In 1860 the Rifle Volunteers were formed—the forerunner of today's Territorial Army. Uneasiness as to French intentions after the formation of the Russo-French Alliance had led to rifle-clubs being organised all over the country. The Corn Hall was put to good use as the drill hall for the 30-strong

53 Etching of St Nicholas' church, showing the old Bath House (on the left) before it was pulled down in 1855.

54 The Corn Exchange, opened in 1857.

Dereham Company. Although the Volunteers never fired a shot in anger, the Company quickly became an important addition to the town's social life. Armstrong's diary makes this clear:

September 22nd 1863. A grand entertainment to the Dereham and Wymondham Volunteers at Letton Hall. A vast crowd was assembled. An elegant repast was provided for the guests in the dining room, and the Volunteers, about 150 in number, sat down to an excellent dinner under a tent. The speeches were unusually good, especially those of Lord Woodhouse and Robert Gurdon who is Captain of the Wymondham Corps. Capt Bulwer replied for the Derehamites. The band played at intervals. What a wonderful change all this is! Here is a new source of interest - a new bond of fellowship —and appliances for pleasure, and festivity, which were not in existence ten years ago.

Drills were held in the Corn Hall. The first uniforms were grey, later changed to red. Rifle shooting was carried out on a range at Swanton Morley; old maps show the site as being on the meadows behind the church. Evidently members were recruited from a wide area round Dereham, as in 1861 a silver cup for marksmanship, presented by Mr Freeman of Swanton, was won by a young tanner from Worthing. There must have been great keenness in the ranks and wide support from the townspeople, for in September 1861 the Dereham Company were sufficiently well-trained to take part in a review at Holkham Hall. A Public Holiday was declared, all the shops closed, and 6,000 people travelled by Eastern Counties Railway excursion trains to see the fun. From its inception, Parson Armstrong was an enthusiastic supporter of the Company, for at heart he seems to have been a frustrated field-marshal. On 13 January 1855 he wrote:

My cousin, Henry Armstrong, is gazetted first lieutenant of his regiment. I remember the time when I should have jumped at such a chance; and even now, next to what I am, were I a few years younger and single, I should prefer the Army to all other professions.

55 Norfolk jacket.

And so, when in 1866 he was appointed chaplain to the Dereham Volunteers, his cup of happiness was filled to overflowing. He could wear a uniform and march with the men, when in that year they formed a Guard of Honour for the Prince of Wales, the Duke of Edinburgh and the Queen of Denmark who passed through Dereham. From then on there were frequent references to full-dress military dinners at the vicarage and other residences in the town (officers only, of course), though on more than one occasion he dined both officers and men at the *King's Arms*. They took their part-time soldiering very seriously in those days. When you died you received a full blown military send-off.

Armstrong - October 26th, 1863:

Military funeral of one of the Volunteers, being the first since the formation of the Corps. The officers and men attended in full uniform, drums muffled and the band played the Dead March. At the conclusion 3 vollies were fired over the grave. There were many thousands to see so novel a sight hereabouts —so that Anthony Dye, Plumber and Glazier of East Dereham was more honoured in death than ever he was in life.

The pace and variety of life in the town was now increasing. This happy little picture of an annual event was given by Armstrong in 1861:

July 29th—The annual school feast—the one day of all others in the year when one is anxious for a real fine day. This was fortunately everything one could wish, which was the more fortunate because up to last evening very heavy rains had fallen daily for some time accompanied by thunder and lightning whereby horses were struck and oaks shivered to pieces. But this was a Herbert's day, 'so calm, so cool, so bright'. The proceedings began with a Church service at 3, attended by the children, 350 in number who afterwards went to the old Theatre (recently converted into St Nicholas Hall) in which tables were set out containing 25 children each, each table being provided by a lady at her own expense, and presided over by her. The eating and drinking, which took a long time, being over, the children proceeded in order to the Vicarage 'the scene of so many festive and happy gatherings' as the paper said, and then spent the evening in various sports. About 1000 people were in the grounds, and the Rifle Band played at intervals till dark affording the opportunity for dancing in which young and old, rich and poor, joined. Subscribers were entertained with refreshments within the vicarage and the proceedings terminated with a fire-balloon which ascended beautifully in the calm evening air. Altogether we never had a more successful gathering and the visitors repeatedly expressed their gratification.

On another occasion, he attended a concert and recorded this fine description of those present:

Took my little girls to a concert given by my organist Mr Martin, at which Miss Alleyne and Miss Lizzy Stuart sang. I was amused how 'humbug' was reigning supreme on this occasion. Thus the giver of the concert styles himself as 'Professor Martin' and Herr Rust, of Her Majesties private Band is no other, notwithstanding his moustache and well-cut clothes, than plain Bill Rust of Dereham whose father shoes horses and whose mother sells cakes and fruit. Moreover he is said not to be connected with Her Majesty except as a private and loyal subject. Then there was Lieut Hill the ci-devant Guardsman twisting his moustache at Miss Lee-Warner whose heart he is unable to subdue and there was young Mr Goldson the Lawyer improving the occasion with regard to the pretty Miss Robbards, and there was the beautiful Kate Girling without any lover in an obscure little nook all to herself.

56 The Norfolk-built Burrell-Boydell horse-steered steam-engine, 1858.

57 An Edwardian Friendly Society procession.

On 9 July 1862 the Norfolk Agricultural Show was held in Dereham for the first time. It had not yet become 'Royal' and, in those days, moved round the county until it found a permanent home at Costessey. According to Armstrong, it was held on two fields near the station. One of the exhibits was a four-furrow steam plough, a far cry from the days when the appearance of a horse-powered threshing machine would provoke riots. Among those present were Mr Bagge, MP, Lords Sondes, Hastings and Walsingham, Howes MP, Bentinck MP, Sir W. Jones, the Hon. W. Coke and Gurdon MP. The Show wound up with a display of fireworks in the market place and with the volunteer band—'thus ended a day of the greatest pleasure and excitement'.

The next year saw another day of pleasure and excitement when to mark the wedding of the Prince of Wales, a roast beef feast was provided in the market place for 2,082 poor people (10 March) and on 1 July of that year the newly formed Horticultural Society held its first exhibition, at the Corn Hall.

On 19 May 1864, the annual review of the Battalion of Volunteers was held at Dereham. The Lynn, Holt, Fakenham, Swaffham, Aylsham and other companies joined with Dereham for the review by Lord Suffield, who came here again the next year to meet the Prince and Princess of Wales off the train and to drive them to Gunton. The town was lavishly decorated, triumphal arches were erected and flowers were festooned everywhere, guns were fired and bells rung. The Prince and Princess paid us another visit in 1866 as already mentioned. In 1867 Armstrong wrote:

> January 10th.—The gayest week, perhaps, ever known in Dereham. Volunteers gave two theatrical representations, the bachelors gave a ball, and there was the annual distribution of prizes to the Volunteers.

On 12 June of that year the Dereham Races were held and on 12 September the Dereham Horticultural Society held its annual show, this time at Elmham Park. Lord Sondes of Elmham Hall was active in Dereham affairs, and co-operated with Armstrong in forming such local organisations as the Savings Bank and the Mechanics' Institute. When the Freemasons formed

58 (Opposite, top left) M.U.I.O.O.F. contribution card, 1920.

59 (Opposite, top right) M.U. contribution card, 1920.

60 (Opposite right) Market Place, with sheep pens.

EAST DEREHAM DISTRICT
M.U.I.O.O.F.

LOYAL

"Mary Bulwer" Lodge

No. 3716.

CONTRIBUTION CARD.   No....17....

Sister....G. Reynolds....
....7 Cowper Rd E.D.....

NOTE.—Any member changing her
residence must, within one month inform the Lodge Secretary of her new
address.

No Money received without this Card,
nor after 9.30 p.m.

No Sick Allowance will be paid by the
Sick Visiting Officer until this card is
produced for her inspection.

BRO. F. W. COUNT, TYP., DEREHAM.

EAST DEREHAM DISTRICT, M.U.

LOYAL

"Feeling Heart" Lodge,

No. 2775.

Bro........Reg. James........

No........911........

Monthly Contribution........2/2

Contribution Card

SICK VISITING OFFICERS.

Bro. A. Barkway, 4 St. Nicholas' St., Dereham.
  „ Thos. Mack, 38, Norwich Road,   „
  „ W. F. Fenner, Cowper Road,   „
  „ R. H. Large, Swanton.

Secretary's Address—W. RABY,
    4 Commercial Rd., Dereham.

WERRY, PRINTER, DEREHAM.

Manchester Unity .·. .

Independent Order

. . . . of Oddfellows.

Approved Society No. 123.

80th Balance Sheet

OF THE LOYAL

'Feeling Heart' Lodge

No. 2775, East Dereham District,

HELD AT THE

"LORD NELSON" INN, EAST DEREHAM.

Abstract of Receipts and Disbursements

For the Year ending December 31st, 1921.

LODGE OFFICERS for 1922:—

R. J. SEABROOK, G.M.   H. T. TIMBERS, N.G.   A. E. DACK, V.G.

Treasurers—Messrs. BARCLAY & Co.

Sick Visiting Officers—A. BARKWAY, 4 St. Nicholas Street.
THOS. MACK, 38 Norwich Road.
W. F. FENNER, Cowper Road.   R. H. LARGE, Swanton.

Surgeons—J. K. HOWLETT, Esq., V. J. DUIGAN, Esq. and
D. TURNER BELDING, Esq.

Trustees—HENRY T. PRECIOUS, GEORGE J. FROST,
J. K. HOWLETT, A. RUSTON, G. W. PELLS and P. H. MACK.

Secretary—WILLIAM RABY, 4 Commercial Road.

Assistant Secretary—GEORGE WRIGHT, Scarning Road.

GEO. COLEBY, PRINTER, DEREHAM.

61 Balance sheet of the Manchester Unity Independent Order of Oddfellows.

62 The old National
School, Cemetery Road,
1841.

62 The old National School, Cemetery Road, 1841.

a lodge here in 1863, they did him the honour of naming it the Sondes Lodge. The Freemasons, with their clandestine activities, contributed little to the overt social scene, but other organisations now springing up were active and prominent. They were the Friendly Societies, formed to help their members, mainly working men, in times of unemployment and sickness. They paraded with bands, banners and regalia, especially at Whitsun which had become a very festive time in the town.

But we must leave the giddy whirl of social life in the 1860s and consider more mundane things. The Education Act of 1870 provided School Boards to ensure that all children had the opportunity of education. The Dereham Board was formed in 1872, and decided that three new schools were needed; at Toftwood, Etling Green and in the town. The old British and Infants' School in London Road was adapted to meet the town's needs, and was available for occupation in 1873. The Toftwood and Etling Green schools were opened in 1875. The status of the National School remained unaltered, much to Armstrong's delight.

He was less than delighted in 1874, when he attended a meeting to discuss the letting of Rush Meadow for growing water cress:

March 18th: Last night I attended the most 'rowdy' and uproarious meeting ever assembled in Dereham. The case was this : a tract of land called 'Rush Meadow' is open to the poor as a fuel allotment, on which they may cut sedge-grass and turf. But it is almost always under water and the sedge valueless, the poor do not think it worth while to go for it. A London man has offered the Vicar and Churchwardens, who are the trustees, no less than £40 a year for this swamp, to grow water-cresses to be sent to London— the only purpose for which it is worth anything, except for snipe and occasional wild duck. There is also a considerable and larger portion which is not to be parted with, and which has fair pasture. The £40 we proposed to spend annually in coals for the poor, thus converting the useless sedge into fuel worth having. It seems, however, that a number of horse-dealers, 'dicky' buyers, fish-cart people and hucksters are not only in the habit of turning their animals on to this tract, but of receiving payment for turning on the cattle of people who do not even belong to the parish. Some of these men are well off and one of them we know to be worth £1000, whereas, legally, people are ineligible for pasturage who have £15 a year. The whole thing, in short, is a gross abuse.

A meeting was called by these gentry to protest against the action of the trustees, and Churchwarden Carthew and myself attended. We found the room full of 'roughs', and the chair was taken by W. who was perfectly incapable of keeping order. I endeavoured to address the meeting to explain the case, but they only gave a partial hearing, interrupting by groans, cheers, counter-groans and cheers. But, though I 'said my say' it was of no avail; they had made up their minds to 'no enclosure' and the meeting ended in disorder. Fortunately about half a dozen young fellows came with a view to protect me from the mob, who, as we left St Nicholas's Hall, hooted and yelled therefrom to the Market Place, where the churchwarden and I took refuge in the Reading Room, and afterwards got safely home. But this was not all: Everington, the other churchwarden and trustee (who was not at the meeting, and who was most unpopular because they thought that he wanted the land) happened to drive through the Market Place at 9 p.m. just as the mob let me go. He was driving tandem, and his wife was with him. The mob got round him and so alarmed the horses that they took fright, though happily without accident. Although I went as the real friend of the poor, and do not regret explaining matters, this is the first time that I found myself 'molested', as the Norfolk paper describes me to have been; and certainly unpopular. The respectable portion of the inhabitants are very angry at our treatment.

Perhaps this protest reflects the rising tide of democracy, for only the poorer people benefited from the common rights of Rush Meadow, and they were no longer prepared to defer to their 'betters'. Was Armstrong, like his predecessor Wollaston, about to be overwhelmed by changing times? (See Appendix III.) Rule by an oligarchy consisting of the vicar, the squire, and a few influential gentlemen was coming to an end.

Joseph Arch, the pioneer trade union leader, was holding meetings in the Corn Hall and in 1873 William Lane was appointed a full-time union official and organiser of the Dereham branch of the Agricultural Workers Union. On 4 April 1877 this union attempted to get one of its members into the Vestry but Armstrong declined their request that the meeting should be adjourned to 7 p.m. for the convenience of working men on the grounds that this would cause great inconvenience to other ratepayers. However, their chance to have a say in affairs came that year when the parish was constituted a local government district and an elected Local Board was formed. Not exactly successfully, it would appear from Armstrong's comment on 3 March 1879:

63   Water tower, 1889.

Was elected member of our Local Board, which has, hitherto, been in quite wrong hands, the members doing nothing but quarrel and abuse on another, till at length half of them resigned. Among those elected were Capt. Bulwer, Mr H. Cooper and Dr Vincent, all of whom have, up to the present, held aloof from it.

The Old Guard, wearing different hats!

In 1879 the fire brigade was formed, and in 1892 they bought a steam fire engine, since by this time there was adequate water available for it to pump—which brings us to the sore point of the Water Works. As early as 1854 the Vestry had debated supplying the town with water and thoroughly draining it. This was turned down; we might have had to wash more often! It was not until 1881 that the Water Works was completed and a sewage system provided—but not without

64 Pump.

opposition, for the 'Keep Dereham Dry' campaigners were still active. They displayed these anti-water posters round the town:

Ratepayers of East Dereham.

The Rural Sanitary Authority, without your consent, has taken the Government of your Town!

A sum of £15,000 has been borrowed for Drainage and Water Works.

The Civil Engineer, upon whose report authority has been obtained to proceed with these Works, estimated the cost as follows:-

For Sewage Works, Town Proper	£5,000
" " " Out Town	£2,000
Water Works	£5,700
	£12,700

The sum borrowed is £15,000!! an increase upon the estimated cost of £1,300.

What sum of money will be demanded of you to pay for these schemes which are being forced upon you? Observe, to repay principal and interest in 30 years, etc., etc., you will have to pay £33,450!! for a dangerous experiment and a deadly nuisance. But this only the beginning of the mischief, and only a portion of the expense ...

Beyond the proposed Public Works, every Owner and Occupier may be required to drain his house and premises into the New Sewers: this would involve putting up a Water Closet, and that again a Cistern for Water, and an adequate water supply to cleanse the Closets and to assist the flushing of the Sewers. What will it cost you to alter your present Drains, to construct new ones, to provide Water Closets and Cisterns to all your houses, and for Annual Rate for Water Supply?

What will you lose in Trade by the roads and approaches to your Town being blocked for six months?

Add these items to the £33,450 certain costs and the £24,450 probable cost and say: ...

Will you permit Rush Meadow to be taken possession of, or other land so near to the town, to be flooded with sewage, made an open cesspool, a reeking bed for the generation of Miasma to contaminate your now healthy town?

Will you allow your immemorial right to Local Self-Government to be taken from you, and your money by tens of thousands of pounds, while your very lives are endangered?

   Your fellow townsmen,

W Freeman   E Barwell.

Their campaign was unsuccesful, and eventually water was flowing into every house—in the town, at any rate. Out in the country it took many more years before the pumps, wells and buckets could be dispensed with.

In 1882 the 'Round-the-World' railway line from Norwich to Dereham via Aylsham and Reepham finally reached Dereham. A new station was built between North Elmham and Ryburgh to serve the new county school. This school no doubt brought additional trade to Dereham, but it was not a success and later became the Watts Naval Training School, a branch of Dr Barnardo's. The little lads in their sailor uniforms were a familiar sight in Dereham on Saturday afternoons during the 1930s.

By now Bank Holidays and weekly half-days had been introduced—more free time for sport and recreation. The Dereham Town Football Club was formed in 1884, probably the first organised sport for working people. Cricket in those days was played largely by 'gentlemen' and the other pastimes of the period were hardly suitable for the 'poor'. There was, for instance croquet played at the vicarage, 'a sort of lawn billiards played with a long handled mallet', and archery had become popular among the gentry. In 1877 Armstrong mentions lawn tennis being played at the vicarage. Cycling was becoming established towards the end of the century, but this too began as a middle class recreation. Armstrong was visited in 1869 by his nephew, a naval officer, riding a bicycle. In 1889 J.J. Wright opened a cycle shop, which evidently prospered, for ten years later he was dealing in motor cars. An annual event which brought prestige to the town was the Mid-Norfolk and East Dereham Athletic and Military Festival founded by Thomas Cranmer, a local auctioneer. There were valuable prizes to be won and competitors came from as far afield as London and Liverpool, though evidently there was athletic talent available in Dereham, since a newspaper article of 1888 mentions a Mr Kerrison of Baxter Row, Dereham running from St Benedict's Gates, Norwich to the Easton Dog and back—11 miles in 55 minutes.

Another important local event which owed its inception to the indefatigable Tom Cranmer was the East Dereham Stallion Show, held annually, which attracted a large number of visitors and entries. In 1892, for instance, at the seventh annual show, no less than 66 of these noble animals were on display.

Whilst on the subject of horses it is interesting to recall that we once had a notable member of 'The Turf' in these parts. She was mentioned by Armstrong on 1 July 1875:

> Called out to take a private Baptism at Gorgate, at the extreme end of the parish. The child was an infant who had been deserted in London, and which Mrs Willins of Gorgate, having no children of her own, had brought into Norfolk and adopted, though she is entirely ignorant of its parentage.

66 *Royal Standard*, Baxter Row in the early 1900s.

The child was baptised George William Simpson Willins and was literally cradled in luxury. This good-hearted woman is a very queer one—dresses almost like a man; commits assaults on her grooms; keeps a racer or two, and is well known at Newmarket, Ascot and Epsom as 'Croppy' by reason of her hair being cut quite close to the head!

Good-hearted indeed she was, for the story is told that she would frequently buy the gallery seats at the Dereham Theatre and throw them open to all-comers free of charge, on the principle of 'first come—first served'. With her face wreathed in smiles she would stand in the roadway and watch the struggle among her guests to secure the best seats. Sometimes as a special attraction her little racing pony 'The Maid of Trent' would appear in a drama, *The Flying Squad*.

In 1893 Mr Richard Mayes, a local builder, built a swimming pool and public baths. Despite being opened by Col. Bulwer, with the Temperance Brass Band in attendance, it did not prosper. The silly man should have known better than to expect Dereham people to endanger their lives by going near such a deadly nuisance! The pool was later converted into four houses in what is now called Bath Avenue in Norwich Road. In 1895 the Recreation Ground was opened by Col. Hyde. It became the venue of many local attractions, an early one being a parachute descent from a balloon. The parachutist missed the 'Rec' and came down in a turnip field on the other side of the road—there were fewer houses around then.

In 1888 our much loved vicar resigned through ill-health. The last entry in his diary reads:

May 12th 1887 - It is a long time since I made an entry - partly from failing health and partly from the absence of anything to record.

He was replaced by the Rev. H.J.L. Arnold, and died in 1890. He must surely have been greeted on the other side with the words: 'Well done, thou

67 Hobbies' fire, 28 February 1907.

good and faithful servant'. Armstrong was the last of our vicars to gallop round the parish on a high-mettled nag—even Canon Boston had to make do with a moped!

Gradually the pattern of the town's life was merging into what we know today. In 1894 the East Dereham Urban District Council was formed, and in 1897 H.J. Skinner and Co. joined with 'Hobbies Weekly' to form Hobbies Ltd., one of the largest employers in the town. The Football Club had become well established, and in 1891 its officials were:

President	General Bulwer
Captain	Rev. W.H. Ainger
Secretary	D. Turner Belding
Asst. Secretary	H.C. Simpson
Ground	Rooks Field
Colours	Black and White
No. of Members	57

So, with a general as President, a clergyman as Captain and a doctor as Secretary it would seem that football had not yet acquired its cloth cap image. The population in 1891 was 5,524. In 1897 our durable queen celebrated her Diamond Jubilee. In the market place 3,100 poor people were given a free dinner. To contribute to this festive occasion the clock in the newly-completed tower of the Cowper Church chimed the National Anthem, 'Home Sweet Home', and the 'Blue Bells of Scotland' (according to a local diarist).

There was a fiery end to the century. On 15 August 1899 a blaze at the premises of Thomas Wright in the High Street caused damage of £1,000, and in December the premises of M.F. Vincent, 'Free Trade House' in Swaffham Road, was also extensively damaged.

Chapter VII

Dissent and Diaspora

Before we carry our story forward into the 20th century, let us consider two subjects important enough to warrant a separate chapter—religion and emigration. Religion, in the 19th century, was a growth industry: sects proliferated, much to the dismay of our worthy vicar, the Rev. C.H. Wollaston, who, after long and peaceful years, found his congregation dwindling and his authority being undermined. He was moved to circularise his parishioners in a letter (See Appendix III) appealing for their support, warning them of 'the torrent which is ready to overwhelm you' and asking them 'to come boldly forward and support your own cause, and maintain the religious establishment of your forefathers'. He was about as successful as King Canute, for the 1851 Religious Census, taken on 30 March shows the extent of support the Dissenters had by then been able to command.

Primitive Methodist Chapel, erected 1849.

	AM	PM	Evening
General	34	113	107
Sunday School	70	74	
Totals	104	187	107

Particular Baptist, established 60 years and upwards.

	AM	PM	Evening }
General	93	152	Minister }
Sunday School	55	52	absent no }
Totals	148	204	services }

The Independent Chapel, erected 1815.

	AM	PM	Evening
General	138	74	186
Sunday School	98	115	
Totals	236	189	186

The Church of Jesus Christ of the Latter Day Saints—Building erected about 1800 (it was formerly the Workhouse).

	AM	PM	Evening
General	13	30	0
Sunday School	0	0	0
Total	13	30	0

The Wesleyan Methodist Chapel, erected 1824.

	AM	PM	Evening
General	0	65	54
Sunday School	0	9	0
Totals	0	74	54

Primitive Methodists—Etling Green—(Held in part of a dwelling house.)

	AM	PM	Evening
General	30	40	0
Sunday School	25	0	0
Totals	55	40	0

Statistics for the parish church were not given but it was estimated that attendances were split evenly between the church and the Dissenters.

Parson Armstrong arrived in 1850 and threw all his youthful energy and enthusiasm into winning back support for the Church. He was a tremendously hard worker and from occasional references in his diary it appears he was successful.

In 1858 he mentioned meetings held in the Corn Exchange by Dissenters 'who have closed their meeting houses', and later wrote about 'Sunday preachings in the Corn Exchange which I find are chiefly attended by the poor from distant parishes attracted by a brilliantly lighted room with a fire'. There is something rather touching about this picture of people tramping through the dark along lonely roads and muddy lanes just to experience for a brief hour or so the bliss of light and warmth which they probably had little enough of at home in deep mid-winter.

Armstrong, though he strove mightily on behalf of the church, did not seem to be entirely hostile to his rival clerics, and mentions his encounters from time to time in a tolerant, sometimes even admiring way:

November 11th, 1861 - During an afternoon's visitation with curate fell in with a pious old Baptist local preacher, very poor, teetotaller and only tastes meat when, sent to some local village, he dines with some member of his sect. The good old man lives quite alone, a hermit sort of life, his only companion being his Bible. Gave him a trifle.

68 (Below left) Methodist church, Norwich Road.

69 (Below right) Baptist church, High Street.

Armstrong was undoubtedly impressed by the Mormon missionary he met by chance on Northall Green on 4 March 1854:

> To make up for yesterday visited all the small farms and cottages on Northall Green. I often think and circumstances seem to bear out the supposition, that one's footsteps seem specially guided on such occasions. Thus in a certain cottage I was expostulating with the inmate on the absurdity of Mormonism to which she had addicted herself, when a fine tall young fellow entered the room with a good-natured and amiable smile, said, 'Well sister, how are you'. He was dressed in a green shooting coat, pink cheque (sic) shirt open at the throat, and had a carpet-bag slung over his shoulder by means of a stick. What was my surprise to find that this truly un-ecclesiastical character was a veritable Mormon Elder and that Mrs Butters, the owner of the cottage was his sister 'In the Lord'. Of course we got to polemics, in which he maintained that no Ministry was genuine which could not work miracles, and cited the 'signs' which our Lord said, should follow 'them that believed'. On my saying that on seeing a miracle worked before my eyes I might believe it, he replied that it could not be done without I had previous faith. I said that if I had such faith, he would reply that there was no need of a miracle and that moreover the miracle of our B.L. and his Apostles were worked before the unbelieving. He said they were only done by Xt for the benefit of the particular person interested. Mrs Butters, however, struck in by saying she had been the subject of a miracle. It appears that she had so bad a sore throat that, to use her words, 'it was swelled on a level with her chin, but that it was healed in less than five minutes by the prayer of a Mormon Elder'. I had nothing to say to this, altho' I might have added a Popish miracle, narrated to me by Mr Capes, who says a certain Captain of Dragoons was cured of Elephantiasis by the application of a relic. This he told me himself. To return to the Mormon; he advocated a plurality of wives, denied (?) infant baptism and maintained that God the Father had 'parts and passions'. He seemed thoroughly in earnest, and was by no means wanting in shrewdness. About two hours after our meeting in the cottage I encounterd him trudging on the road, and we had ten minutes more chat. He said his sphere of labour comprised about $\frac{1}{4}$ of the county of Norfolk, and that in it were about 150 Mormons. He lived on what the faithful chose to give him, and prided himself on being exactly like the original disciples because he had 'neither purse nor scrip'. He seemed surprised when I told him that according to that rule he ought not to have 'shoes' either. This is a sad delusion, but the preposterous claims it makes proportionally incline the ignorant to it. The dissenters and low church are very irate against the poor Mormons but for my own part, I do not see they are worse than other dissenters. In fact they retain some (?) notions of Catholic truth beyond other schismatics. The written account of their migration to Salt Lake is wonderful and reminds one in some particulars of the Exodus of the Israelites.

It is an unfortunate fact that in those days the rival sects did tend to become rather 'irate' with one another, and physical violence cannot altogether be ruled out.

The Norfolk Constabulary was formed in 1840 under Colonel Richard Montague Oakes, and, new and inexperienced though it was, seems to have quickly earned the confidence of the public, for in the minutes of the quarterly meeting of the Mattishall Methodist Circuit in 1841 is recorded:

> It is resolved that Etling Green camp meeting be removed to Neatherd providing that Carnal Okes will send in the police to protect us.

No doubt a rabble could be relied upon to congregate at the drop of a hat to make trouble for any new organisation appearing on the streets. It happened when in 1883 a detachment of the Salvation Army came to Dereham to carry out 'an assault and bombardment against the Citadel of sin'. They marched, stoutly honking and thumping, through the town, with their inveterate antagonists, the 'Skeleton Army', snapping at their heels. Between them they kicked up such a racket that the good folk of Dereham could get no sleep and, once again, the police had to be called upon to restore order. The Skeleton Army was a gang of hoodlums intent upon breaking up the S.A. meetings. On the principle of 'why should the Lord have all the best hymns?', they composed a parody of the Salvationist hymn:

> Turn to the Lord and seek salvation,
> Praise the sound of His dear name ...

Their version ran something like this:

> Turn to the wall and seek fat spiders,
> Sing the praise of their long legs,
> Go to the shop and buy a pound of bacon,
> It'll go well with their fried legs!

The Salvationists are still with us, but the Skeleton Army has long since disappeared—there must be a moral somewhere!

It was not just for attendance at services that the two sides were in competition. The Dissenters seemed to maintain the attitude, 'anything you can do we can do better'. They opened a rival school, 'The British and Infants' to compete with the Church 'National' School. Mr W.W. Lee-Warner was a patron of this, his attitude was somewhat ambiguous, and is nicely summed up by Armstrong as 'undulating gently between Church and Dissent'. Despite his support for the Dissenters' School, he has a memorial in the parish church.

It appears that 'poaching' of supporters was not unknown. For instance on 2 November 1853, we find Armstrong 'Employed the afternoon in looking up several children who had left the school and found that certain dissenters had agreed to pay for them if, they went to the "British and Foreign"'[sic].

Public Lectures were popular in Victorian times. They were another source of inter-denominational rivalry. For instance, on 23 January 1861,

> Rev. Morgan lectured at the Institute on Greece. Room half full due to one
> 'Jabez Inwards Esq.,' lecturing at the Corn Hall under the presidency of one
> of our dissenting ministers.

70 The National School, 1841.

There was even competition in the field of charity work:

January 3rd, 1860 :- 'District Visiting Society and Clothing Club all the morning. The sub-committee for collecting subscriptions giving in their report it was found we are ably supported as ever not-withstanding the opposition Society consisting of the Dissenters and Low Church.'

Even in death the sects were divided. When the new cemetery came into use in 1869 God's acre was partitioned into two half-acres, each with its own mortuary chapel—Church of England on the right, The Rest on the left. These two chapels are identical, built to a design by Browne of Norwich in the Early English style, with plentiful insertions of coloured bricks—but what a waste of money!

Armstrong recorded the event:

November 1st, 1869—

This was the day fixed by the Bishop for the consecration of Dereham cemetery. I met his lordship at the station at 1.13 and drove him to the National School, which is contiguous to the cemetery and made an excellent vestry. A procession was then formed, which proceeded round the ground singing "Brief life is here our portion". It drizzled all the time ... I was very thankful when the day was over.

Whether adherence to one sect was always whole-hearted seems doubtful, when one finds an instance of this sort:

A district visitor speaking of some twins I had baptised privately a few days ago expressed her satisfaction to the parents, they being Dissenters. 'Oh' said the man 'I ollus say, begin and end with the Church, whatever you do between-whiles - when it comes to a job of that sort [i.e. baptism or burial] there's nought like the Church.'

The chapels were particularly successful in attracting adherents from the remote parts of the parish. Possibly it was there that they first gained a foothold, for they were careful to give the hamlets special mention in their prayers for blessing on the East Dereham Methodist Church:

'Into Toftwood send Thy power,
Etling Green Thy fulness know.'

It was into Toftwood that Armstrong on 9 December 1852 launched his counter-attack:

Having obtained the use of an empty house and sent on some forms beforehand, started for Toftwood Common at 6, to hold a service and lecture. The poney [sic] cart was loaded with myself and curate, two surplices, 3 choristers, a small lectern, a pound of wax candles, some candlesticks, Bibles, Prayer Books and the dinner bell to call them to Service. For this last, however, there was no need, as upwards of 60 persons were in the room before our arrival and many more were unable to get in.

He did not neglect Etling Green, and frequently mentioned his visits there:

December 16th 1859, The snow so deep and the weather so piercing cold that I drove in a sleigh to Evening Service in the School House at Etling Green, which had not a single track across it. When preaching to these rustics in their working dresses I though how different my company and occupation to that of last evening! [this was a dinner party at the Vicarage] What a contrast between the well got up military guests at the dinner table and these poor fellows ingrained with toil—between the silk and lace crinoline of the ladies and the cotton gown and shawl of the residents of the hamlet! Much as I enjoyed last evening I derived much greater satisfaction from this tho' the cold was 20° below freezing and the water in bedroom ewers was thickly frozen the next morning.

In the face of such zeal it is difficult to imagine how the chapels held on to their followers. Perhaps it was because 'these rustics' would have felt out of place in the Gothic splendour of the church, and preferred the simple and homely surroundings of a tiny chapel. The vicar would have welcomed them as he once wrote:

> Nevertheless I much desire we could get the poor together in church, in their working clothes, and address them familiarly on this subject. Dissenters and Romanists manage this.

The question is—would his congregation have been quite so enthusiastic? Jack Rag and Tom Straw, reeking of the stable and sty, would have mingled uneasily with the eau-de-cologne and lavender water of the prosperous tradesmen and superior artisans of the urban area.

Dr Jessopp, Rector of Scarning, in his book *Arcady: for better or worse*, gave other reasons to account for the popularity of the chapels:

> There is no denying it that in hundreds of parishes in England the stuffy little chapel by the wayside has been the only place where for many a long day the very existence of religious emotion has been recognised; the only place in which the yearnings of the soul and its strong crying and tears have been allowed to express themselves in the language of the moment unfettered by rigid forms; the only place where the agonized conscience has been encouraged and invited to rid itself of its sore burden by confession and comforted by at least the semblance of sympathy; the only place where the peasantry have enjoyed the free expression of their opinions, and where, under an organization elaborated with extraordinary sagacity, they have kept up a school of music, literature and politics, self supporting and unaided by dole or subsidy - above all, a school of eloquence in which the lowliest has been familiarised with the ordinary rules of debate, and has been trained to express himself with directness, vigour and fluency.

These are quite remarkable sentiments for a Church of England clergyman of that time to express, but then, if there is one thing you must expect from Old Jessopp, it is the unexpected.

It is obvious from reading Armstrong's diary that a ding-dong battle was going on to win over the man in the street. He never ceased visiting every house in the town, whatever the persuasion of its occupants, for they were all 'his parishioners'. On 16 July 1852:

> Visited a parishioner of the undoubted age of 102—he has lately been brought to Dereham and is residing with his son, who is a dissenting tailor in the market place, the builder of, and occasionally the preacher in, a Meeting House—best remembered is his own 'conversion' which he describes as having occurred on the occasion of hearing a non-conformist sermon at Shipdham in the 32nd year of his age. Gave him my priestly blessing.

In passing, we could mention that ripe old age was quite a feature of the town. The bracing air of Arcady, perfumed by the privies, the pigsties and the steaming piles of horse manure was conducive to longevity in the days before new-fangled hygienic notions like hot baths and water closets came along to undermine a man's constitution. The old gentleman in question died at the age of 104. The same year Mr Barry Girling died at 92. In 1870 Mrs

Sally Gooch, lady of the manor of Mowles alias Colbournes, died aged 98—'she had never had a day's illness, or knew what pain was'. In the same year Mr T. Harvey died aged 91.

In 1879 a Mr Cooper died, aged 91. He waited on Lord Nelson and Lady Hamilton on the evening when Nelson was summoned to join the Fleet for Trafalgar, and also remembered the midnight funeral of William Cowper.

On 7 July 1888, Samuel Bates died aged 99. He was the son of the 104-year-old gentleman mentioned by Armstrong, and had built the meeting house in Norwich Street, now used as the Masonic Hall.

In 1881, Mary Martin died, aged 98. She remembered the French prisoner escaping from the 'Clocker' and being shot—'up Sandy Lane', she said, but this is debatable. An interesting pencilled note in the margin of a copy of Carthew's *History of Dereham* in the Norwich Local Studies Library reads: 'He ran up the lane leading past Rush Meadow and climbed a tree which stood in the meadow on the right just before you come to the bridge over the stream. So Mr Barry Girling said who must have well remembered it.'

The opportunities for emigration, offered as our overseas Colonies expanded, were siezed upon eagerly, and we find Dereham people at the utmost ends of the Earth. This was the time of the great British diaspora when English became the most wide-spread language in the world, and Kipling was able to write:

> Never was isle so little,
> never was sea so lone
> But over the scud and the palm trees,
> an English flag was flown.

Adventurous Dereham men (and women) went abroad, some as Service men, some as settlers; and far-away places became commonplace names in the newspapers and in the indispensible Armstrong diaries.

This notice appeared in the *Norfolk Chronicle*, 18 December, 1830:

Died on 4th July last, at Sincapore, Captain William Howard, son of Mr William Howard, of East Dereham.

Australia seems to have been a favourite destination for Dereham emigrants. Perhaps they were influenced by a lecture given in 1859 by a Mr Wigg, who had returned home after seven years there, and who evidently prospered, since he presented the Cowper Congregational Church with its parsonage, built in St Withburga Lane. On 20 July 1860 Armstrong recorded:

Called on Dr Warcop to condole him on the death of his only son in Melbourne—his son was a chaplain RN.

On 29 July the same year:

Published banns of marriage for George Dove—my dear curate, who has accepted an SPG chaplaincy in Adelaide.

November 16th, 1861:
Some aged people told me their daughter who had emigrated to Adelaide was a member of Dove's congregation there.

March 16th, 1862:
Visited a poor heart-broken woman who has taken to her bed and refuses to be comforted for the absence of her children gone to the Colonies.

August 16th, 1859:

Sent a packet of prayers to one of my old National Scholars who is married and settled in Australia.

June 27th, 1853:

Mr Parkerson, our doctor and his family of 8 sons and 4 daughters left us yesterday for the Canterbury settlement, New Zealand.

Armstrong recorded two remarkable anecdotes concerning emigration; one an outstanding success, the other an ignominious failure ending in tragedy:

February 11th, 1854:

Mr Jas Chambers went out in 1836 from East Dereham to Australia, under the auspices of the Emigration Commissioners. Such however was his energy of character and aptitude for business that they released him from the engagements. He became the Government Contractor for the delivery of Mails throughout the Colony and also for fetching the Gold escorts from Mt. Alexander, etc. He took to the diggings 100 horses for which he received near £10,000 and thus became one of the most thriving and wealthy men in the Colony. He is in possession of several thousand acres of land - a lead mine of great value - a large property in Adelaide - a flock of 15,000 sheep, a herd of 2000 cattle and about 2000 horses, etc, etc. He has just disposed of his mail and coach establishment for £14,000.

This worthy son of Dereham evidently believed in performing his duties with a flourish. The official *History of the City of Adelaide* gives this description of his arrival there with the first convoy of gold from the Mt Alexander goldfield:

Here the overland armed gold escorts from Mt Alexander, Victoria, ended their journey. The first two arrivals of the gold escorts in Adelaide were festive occasions as crowds of spectators turned out to watch James Chambers driving his convoy through the town streets towards the Treasury at a mad gallop.

A prudent reporter of the South Australian Register ended a long and vivid article about one such occasion with the words:

The finale of the procession was the escorting of Mr Chambers home, which we did not attend, as whether from fatigue or excitement we noticed the lurking devil under "Jemmy's" smugglers cap, and dreaded instinctively that some of the barrels of the revolver, so conspicuously displayed in his belt, might somehow go off, and as it has been said nobody knows who may be shot in a crowd, even though he should be a special reporter.

For all his great wealth and fame, 'Jemmy' did not forget the relatives he left behind in Dereham. There is proof of that in the churchyard where stands a stone in memory of 'Charles, son of Wm and Elizabeth Chambers and Hugh his brother', and engraved: 'This stone is erected by the remaining brothers and sister James John and Priscilla after 20 years absence in the Colonies Adelaide South Australia. August 1855'.

Armstrong followed this with a very different story:

Having to ride to Tuddenham to get off a dinner party at the Rectory on account of the Even-song thought I would make a morning's Parochial work in that part of the Parish. In the course of it, a small farmer told me the following story, of the large part of which I was already aware.

Some time back an old lady bequeathed £126 each to two sisters, parishioners living in Dereham and the money has caused nothing but misery in all directions. Thus a respectable young man who was engaged to marry my excellent little School-mistress at Etling Green, jilted her and married one of the rich sisters. But it is with the other we have chiefly to do. On hearing of her good fortune another young man, as unprincipled as the former was weak, was accepted as her future husband. He persuaded her to transfer ye fatal £126 from the Colchester to the Norwich Bank and accompanied her to the former place to draw it, for that purpose. He had it in sovereigns - and quickly disappeared therewith. Thus the unfortunate girl lost her husband and her money and perhaps more than that. Meanwhile the papers are full of the wreck of an emigrant ship in Dublin Bay in which 400 souls were suddenly called to their last account. Among the names of the deceased was Schilling, who was found with the fatal £126 in <u>sovereigns</u> tied in a bag

United Methodist Church.

EAST DEREHAM CIRCUIT.

RECEIPTS.

Sept., 1911.	C.F.C.		H.H.		Plans		Aug. 4th.			Sept. 4th.			Total.		
	s.	d.	s.	d.	s.	d.	£	s.	d.	£	s.	d.	£	s.	d.
Dereham......	8	0	2	0	1	10	1	13	1½	2	0	1	3	13	2½
Saham.........			4	3	1	0	1	15	0	0	10	0	2	5	0
Longham ...			1	2	1	9	0	10	1½	0	10	6½	1	0	8
Gressenhall					3	0	2	3	6	1	0	0	3	3	6
Litcham	5	0½			2	0				1	7	9½	1	7	9½
Beeston					1	0				1	0	7	1	0	7
Massingham															
Castleacre ...					1	6	1	0	0	0	3	6	1	3	6
Ashill															
Necton			2	0½	1	6				0	15	0	0	15	0
Mileham			2	0	1	0	0	9	0	1	0	6	1	9	6
Wellingham					1	9	0	9	0	0	9	0	0	18	0
Whissonsett					1	0	1	15	3	1	12	0	3	7	3
Shipdham ...						9	2	0	0	1	0	9	3	0	9
	13	0½	11	5½	18	1	11	15	0	11	9	9	23	4	9

By Loan from London and Provincial Bank .. 11 0 0

£34 4 9

PAYMENTS.

	£	s.	d.
Rev. A. J. Keeley's Salary and Book Room Account ...	22	14	0
Rev. A. H. Nicholas' Salary Account	8	7	6
Interest on Necton Chapel	0	17	8
Secretary's Postages	0	3	0
C.F.C. 13/0½, H.H. 11/5½, Plans 18/1	2	2	7

£34 4 9

CIRCUIT'S LIABILITIES.

	£	s.	d.
Bank Loan and Interest	11	6	9
Salary—Rev. A. H. Nicholas	1	0	0
Removal Expenses ditto	4	4	4
Equalization Fund	4	0	0
H.H. Deficiency	0	15	5½
	21	6	6½
Plan Treasurer's Balance in hand	0	4	10½
Total Debt ...	£21	1	8

J. J. HORNE, *Circuit Steward.*

71 United Methodist church receipts list.

round his neck! Yes, it was the same man! Vainly had he endeavoured to recommence life in the New World with ye fruits of his heartless plunder as his stock in trade!

A footnote to this entry, in another hand, reads

Can this ship be the 'Tayleur' wrecked on Lambay Island in 1854, I think?
H.B.J.A. June 19th 1925

Chapter VIII

The 20th Century

We can only sketch the outline of this period, but several excellent booklets have recently been published that give fuller details and many photographs of the early 1900s.

This was the time of the Edwardian summer, a leisurely and gracious era (at least for the well-to-do). During this period the industrial side of Dereham was developing. Hobbies Ltd., founded in 1897, was prospering and would soon become a household name with world-wide branches, selling fretwork tools amd materials. William Crane, a Fransham wagon builder opened a branch at South Green, which before long became his main works. In due course he turned to building trailers for motor vehicles and secured a particularly lucrative contract to build the trailers for the 'mechanical horses' being introduced by the railway companies to replace their horse-drawn delivery vehicles. J.J. Wright, who had opened a cycle shop in 1889, began dealing in the motor vehicles, thus founding another thriving Dereham business.

72 Agricultural market, c.1910.

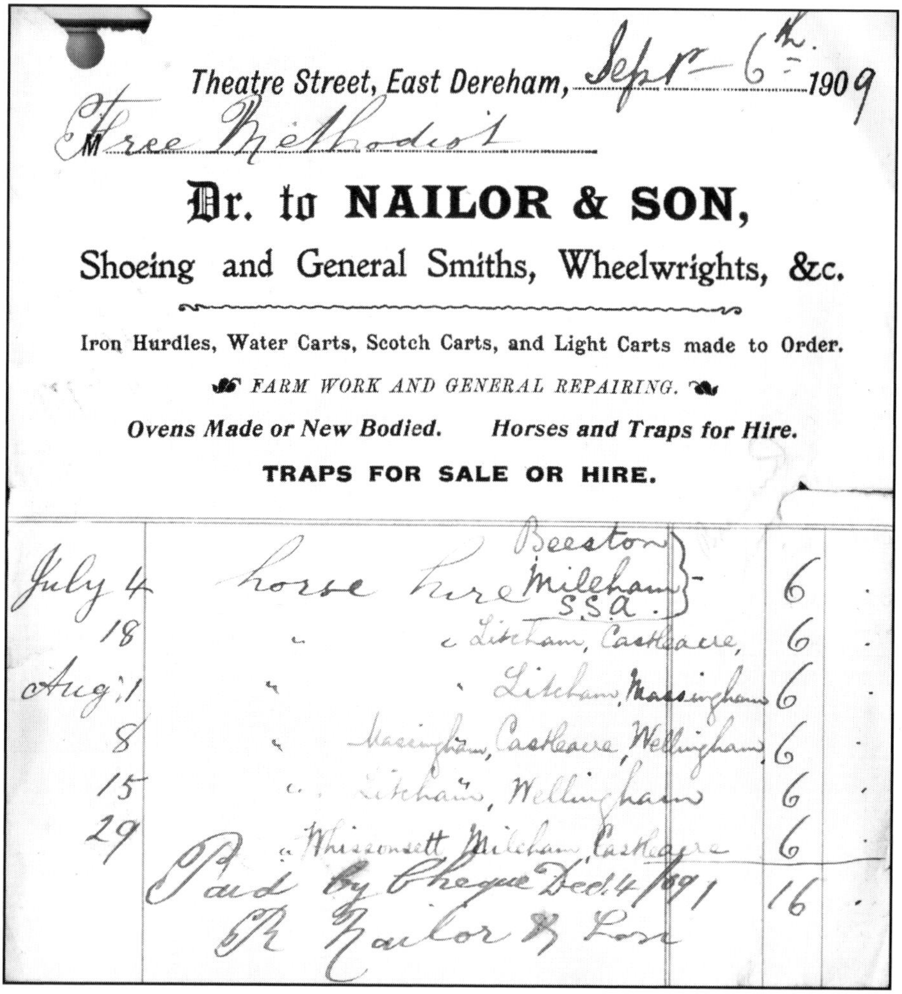

Theatre Street, East Dereham, Sept 6th 1909

M Free Methodist

Dr. to NAILOR & SON,

Shoeing and General Smiths, Wheelwrights, &c.

Iron Hurdles, Water Carts, Scotch Carts, and Light Carts made to Order.

FARM WORK AND GENERAL REPAIRING.

Ovens Made or New Bodied. ***Horses and Traps for Hire.***

TRAPS FOR SALE OR HIRE.

July 4	horse hire Beeston Mileham SSA	6
18	" " Litcham, Castleacre,	6
Aug 1	" " Litcham, Massingham	6
8	" " Massingham, Castleacre, Wellingham	6
15	" " Litcham, Wellingham	6
29	" " Whissonsett Mileham Castleacre	6
	Paid by Cheque Dec 4/09	16
	R Nailor & Son	

73 Invoice for horse hire.

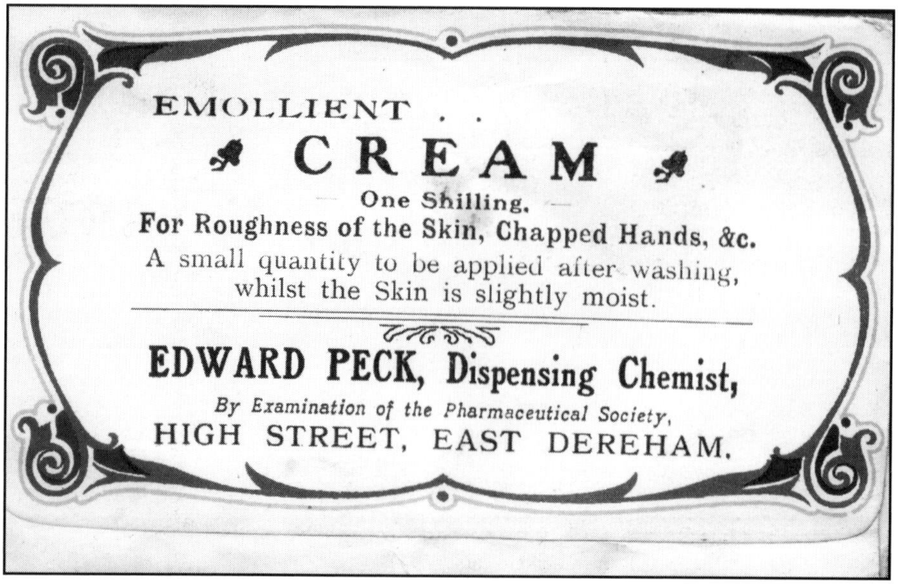

EMOLLIENT . .
CREAM
One Shilling.
For Roughness of the Skin, Chapped Hands, &c.
A small quantity to be applied after washing, whilst the Skin is slightly moist.
EDWARD PECK, Dispensing Chemist,
By Examination of the Pharmaceutical Society,
HIGH STREET, EAST DEREHAM.

74 Emollient cream.

NATIONAL UNION OF RAILWAYMEN
NORWICH No. 2 BRANCH

NEW BANNER FUND

PRICE ONE PENNY

The Perfume with which this card is scented can be procured from all Chemists, Perfumers and Stores

N.U.R. NORWICH BRANCHES.
JUBILEE ANNIVERSARY and
VISIT of Mr. J. H. THOMAS, M.P.
IN AID OF ORPHAN FUND.

Price 1d. each.

PHÚL-NÁNÁ
PERFUME
Bouquet of INDIAN FLOWERS
J. Grossmith & Son
Distillers of Perfumes
NEWGATE St LONDON

SHEM-EL-NESSIM
THE SCENT OF ARABY
J. GROSSMITH & SON
Distillers of Perfumes
NEWGATE ST LONDON

75 Charity tickets sold by the N.U.R.

NATIONAL UNION OF RAILWAYMEN.
HEAD OFFICE:
UNITY HOUSE, EUSTON ROAD,
LONDON, N.W. 1.

MEMBER'S CONTRIBUTION CARD.

Branch No. 3 B.

Dereham _____ Branch

Member ____ James R. E. V.

Address ____ South End

E. Dereham

76 N.U.R. membership card.

77 A market day scene, *c*.1930.

78 Jarred's game and poultry, 39 Quebec Street.

79 (Right) F. Wade & Son, Quebec Street, *c*.1908.

80 (Below) Oldfield & Sons, ironmonger's and hardware stores, 13 Market Avenue, *c*.1929.

81 F.W. Count, bookseller and stationer, High Street, c.1920.

82 Hemmet's, confectioner's. In 1929 it was located at 6 Norwich Street but it later moved to High Street. This could be either!

83 Kingston's grocery shop, corner of High Street and Norwich Street, c.1930.

84 Cooper's the jeweller's, 23 High Street, *c*.1910.

85 Pursey's outfitter's, 15-17 High Street, *c*.1910.

86 Pearl Assurance Co. Ltd., 2 High Street, *c*.1929.

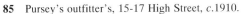

The town was prospering, but all too soon came Armageddon, and the pleasant sun-lit days were over for Dereham men when:

> Shoulder to aching shoulder, side by side
> They trudged away from life's broad wealds
> of light.

It was during the Great War that the town felt the weight of enemy action for the first time in more than 1,000 years. On the night of 8 September 1915, a Zeppelin dropped its bomb load on the Church Street area, causing five deaths and considerable damage.

It is said that when the infernal machine was heard approaching, a quick-witted local man gathered up an armful of hurricane lamps and rushed down to Rush Meadow where he laid them out to make a decoy target. If this is true perhaps we should claim to have created the first 'Starfish' decoy site in the history of aerial warfare. This raid engendered many fine stories —and they lost nothing in the telling. There was, for instance, the pickelhaube (a Kaiser Bill helmet, as one old lady called it) that fell from the clouds. It was picked up and passed round to collect for the victims of the bombs, or, if your head was square, you could be photographed in it for 3d. This seems a rather inprobable item of uniform to be wearing inside a Zeppelin! A more authentic version was given by a 95-year-old lady a few years ago:

> I'll bet there's not another person who saw that Zepp door open and the lights on inside; and saw that figure bring that bomb out! I lay down on the bank opposite the school, I tried to protect the three little children I was with by lying on them. There was dirt flying from the vibration from the Zepp and we were covered with it. The bomb didn't go off and where it landed there was the cap that had been blown off the airman's head. It had a lot of gold braid on it. I put it on my head.

Another story, which seems reliable, was told by an elderly gentleman:

> Harry Alpe, an old boy, was going home and had his old clay pipe knocked out of his mouth, but he wasn't hurt. It frightened him though. There were also some small parachutes found, like a hankie with knots in the corners and strings tied to a piece of calico 4 to 5 inches wide and about 11 yards long, and on the end was a packet of newspapers in German. 'Gott strafe England' was written on the outside.

Dr Howlett ordered that these papers should be baked in the oven in case they had been impregnated with virulent German germs.

Because of wartime censorship the raid was not reported in the newspaper until 1918. It was then that the heroism of a Dereham man was revealed. He was Herbert Leech, a daring draper with a shop in the Market Place. A bomb had ignited Utting and Buckingham's paraffin store nearby and, being too close for comfort to his shop, Mr Leech decided that the fire brigade must be called. Braving the bombs he ran to the *King's Arms* where the maroons used to call out the firemen were kept, only to find that the hotel staff and guests had sought shelter down in the well-stocked cellars. They would not come out (and who could blame them?). Mr Leech thereupon found two maroons and a box of matches and, with the help of a passing soldier, set them off. The resultant explosions caused the Zepp to veer away and the soldier to dive for cover into a cabbage patch; he afterwards decamped at high speed. Anyway, the fire brigade turned out, and eventually got the blaze under control, a task made more difficult by explod-

87 The 5th Battalion Norfolk Regiment, 1914.

88 Off to Dover. The 5th Battalion Norfolk Regiment.

89 The Maltings in the First World War.

ing shotgun cartridges stored in the same building. Mr Leech was complimented for his bravery by military officers and other prominent personages. All in all, a night to remember!

After the Armistice celebrations the town settled down to another pleasant period of further expansion. To its industries were added the East Dereham Foundry, incorporated in 1919, Bowman Models made toy boats and steam engines, Jentique Ltd. made furniture, and Metamec was well known for its electric clocks. A little later, in 1932, the 'Dutch Factory' was opened to make specialist machinery for the expanding sugar beet industry. It was usually referred to thus because its official name 'Dreibholz and Floering' was a little too much for us, though we could sometimes manage 'Dryballs and Florin'!

Perhaps the most noticeable change during the Thirties was the increasing volume of motor traffic. Steam and horse power were being phased out. Soon we could no longer watch Hobbies' horse-drawn 'drug' go plodding past with a load of tree trunks for the sawmill, and the steam engines puffing along pulling showmen's caravans and equipment for Tombland Fair became things of the past. The first traffic lights were introduced on the *King's Head* corner, replacing 'Clockwork Arm', an old fellow who used to stand there wearing a white smock and controlling the traffic with his arms in apparently perpetual motion!

Apart from these changes, things went on much as usual between the Wars. The passing days were marked by Hobbies' powerful hooter sounding the beginning and end of the working day. The weekly market continued to draw crowds from the surrounding villages. Farmers came with their produce, their animals and their wives, and, together with the cattle dealers and what R.H. Mottram called 'rum hoss-dealin' people', filled the streets (and pubs) with a cheerful bustle.

The annual harvest fair came into the market place to relieve the farm worker of some of his hard-earned harvest wages. In those days it had a genuine steam-driven roundabout with fine galloping horses, and much gleaming brass and mirrors. Occasionally a travelling circus would pay us a visit. The Big Top would be erected on the Neatherd, surrounded by animal cages and living quarters for the showmen. As there were no lorries large enough

91 Peace celebrations, 1919.

92 The Cenotaph.

to carry elephants, these patient animals had to trudge, trunk to tail, from town to town.

The Hospital Cup was contested each year on the 'Rec' between two invited football teams. The trophy was displayed on a temporary grandstand (a farm wagon), and was said to be larger than the F.A. Cup. The Hospital Sunday procession would pass through the town on a July Sunday, with its bands and representatives of various organisation. The fire engine was an eye-catching feature, with gleaming scarlet paintwork and polished brass, garlanded with flowers but, alas, no longer pulled by horses. It trundled along behind Walpole & Wright's solid-tyred 3-ton lorry. The procession would end with an open-air service on the Vicarage Meadow.

Once, in the 1930s, we were visited by Alan Cobham's Air Display, a great treat when civil aviation was still in its pioneering days. This display, with its slogan, 'Make the skyways Britain's highways' was intended to popularise flying, and was certainly popular with the younger generation. The aircraft took off from a large field of stubble at Park Farm, Etling Green. The town was also given glimpses of those two famous airships, the R100 and R101, when they passed nearby during their test flights; and once the route of the King's Cup air race took its competitors over the parish.

A less acceptable visitor at that time was Sir Oswald Mosley, who held a rally to drum up support for his Blackshirts—he didn't get much!

Twice during this decade we had royal occasions to celebrate. On 6 May 1935, King George V's Silver Jubilee was marked with the traditional celebrations on the Neatherd, complete with bonfire. Dr Howlett, with his penny-farthing bicycle was much in evidence leading the community

singing. Two years later, also in May, a similar event took place for the coronation of King George VI.

Occasionally the fire engine would be called out. Maroons were fired to warn the firemen, and these aerial explosions (two for a fire in town, three for one out in the country) would frighten the pigeons off the Corn Hall, set firemen in rapid motion towards the fire station and send small boys scampering for their bicycles, for a good fire was a spectacle not to be missed in those pre-television days when entertainment was scanty.

We did, however, have the cinematograph, installed in the converted Corn Hall, and a swimming pool in Norwich Street, in what is now the War Memorial Hall.

Happy days, but they came to an abrupt end on Sunday, 3 September 1939, when all the lights went out.

During the next six years the town's population was swollen by evacuees and Service personnel of the RAF and USAAF and Army units stationed in the neighbourhood. To provide entertainment during the blacked-out evenings, the swimming pool was converted into another cinema and even the old Theatre Royal was pressed into service for yet a third. There was plenty of work for the factories, now busy with government contracts, and a new siding was built at the station to handle the greatly increased volume of military traffic. A booklet is in course of preparation to cover the World War II period in greater detail than we can offer here, so we will pass on to 1945. The post-war years were not kind. Vandals ran riot. The historic old *King's Arms* coaching inn was pulled down to make room for that epitome of modern culture—Woolworths. Then they turned their attention to Becclesgate House, which according to Boston & Puddy in 1952, seemed at one time to stand a chance of survival:

> It is in the air that the Post Office will one day move to Becclesgate House but the Treasury had drawn in its purse strings for the present. Nor will the change-over take place yet to a robot automatic telephone exchange from the present personal and efficient manual service, whose ability to be intelligent is so valuable in emergencies. Long may the change over be delayed.

95 The Post Office, 1907.

Alas! it eventually came: Becclesgate House was demolished to make room for the new Post Office. The mellow old Victorian Post Office came down, too, and in its place has arisen that astonishing edifice—a cross between a carbuncle and a sore thumb—which now stands next door to G.D. Cook's.

On 21 June 1950, the statue of Coke of Norfolk, that doyen of local agriculture, was toppled from his plinth on the Corn Hall during a thunderstorm. It was a delightfully symbolic incident for, soon after, the cattle market was closed and the town eschewed its solid old agricultural heritage. Today it lies under an alien 'loadsamoney' gloss, as uncomfortable as an old farm labourer dolled up in hired finery for a wedding; and Cockney is fast replacing Broad Norfolk in its car-strangled streets. Old family firms closed their doors for the last time—names like Kingston and Hurn, Aldiss and Utting and Buckingham vanished, to be replaced by chain stores and supermarkets, all trying to stamp out our local individuality and turn this old place into yet another Admassville. They have not quite succeeded, for even today it is worth while, on some tranquil summer's evening when the sun is low over Scarning Dale, to walk down Church Street to where it all began; and where the streamlet to which Withburga's does came to drink still flows past the bottom of the churchyard, for something which the ancients called divine will be found and felt there still.

Appendix I

'Who hath stolen our Saint?'

The busy commercial town of Dereham today gives no indication that once this was ground as holy and enchanted as ever was Camelot or Glastonbury. The town was described in Hunt's *Directory* of 1850 thus:

> The great characteristics of this town are—the activity and perseverance of its inhabitants in all measures calculated to promote the public weal —the cleanliness and beauty of its streets—the busy retail trade—its well-attended markets—and the spirit of intelligence which pervades its general society.

How little have we changed over the years!
Unfortunately Mr. Hunt added a less acceptable remark:

> Many idle legends are connected with the early history of East Dereham but these are too gross for belief.

He is referring to the story of our very own St Withburga, and the legends and miracles surrounding her life, death and after. Since Withburga was to Dereham almost what great Diana was to the Ephesians, such a statement is blasphemy indeed. There are many versions of her story, agreeing in broad outline but differing somewhat in detail; which is not surprising since this is a story from long ago, a tale out of the misty dawn of Christianity in our land. 'Gross', maybe, but it is a charming old legend, well worth the telling; for after all, how colourless the past would seem without those golden threads of folklore that run through the sober tapestry of history.

Princess Withburga was the youngest daughter of King Anna of the East Angles, a beautiful maid of studious and religious nature, born of a saintly family into a turbulent half-heathen time. She spent her early years in the coastal village of Holkham where she was held in high esteem for her piety and royal blood and where the church is dedicated to her memory. Upon the death of her father, killed in battle in AD 654, the princess, heartbroken and impoverished, came here intent upon founding a religious house on the last remnant of her father's lands. It must have been a lovely spot in those days, a gentle south facing slope leading down to a streamlet running through shady woods and sunny water-meadows, where wild deer roamed.

What happened then is told in an ancient chronicle written by the monks of Ely:

> This holy virgin in the years of her girlhood, constructed a cell at Dereham and there assumed the habit of a nun. It happened that when she was building a church in that place she had no victuals except dry bread for the workmen; she resorted to the Virgin, her only hope after Christ, for succour, who appeared to her in her sleep, telling her to trust in the Lord, take no care for things of the body nor think of the morrow. 'Send', said she 'early in the morning your maids to the neighbouring bridge over the stream, and there shall meet them every day two does whose milk shall minister to your necessities'. Accordingly next morning she sent her damsels to the bridge,

about a furlong distant, and, behold there met them two does, from milking which the virgins obtained so much milk that two men could scarcely carry the pail upon their shoulders, and they afforded plenty for all. But the bailiff or chief man of the town, a pagan perhaps, divined it, and at length stimulated by indignation brought his dogs and endeavoured to take the deer. But while he was hunting them, and leaping his horse over a fence, the horse fell and the stakes entering his body the rider was thrown backwards and broke his neck. But although deprived of their supply of milk the handmaids of the Lord did not want for sustenance. So, being full of good works she died, having obtained the heavenly palm of virginity and was buried in the churchyard of Dereham.

But that was not the end of the story: the world had by no means heard the last of Withburga. Let the Rev. Benjamin Armstrong, a notable 19th-century vicar of Dereham continue the narrative in his quaint style:

And lo' after many more years had passed, and the other tenants of the churchyard, and even those that had been buried long after, had mouldered into dust, the grave of Withburga being opened, her body was found entire and without the slightest sign of corruption. Aye, there she lay in her shroud and coffin, and with her little crucifix of silver lying upon her breast, even as she had lain on the bier on the day of her death so many, many years before. The saintly incorruptible body was forthwith removed into the church, where it was preserved with great care and devotion by the good people of Dereham, and it continued there not without manifold miracles.

Those miracles were to prove our undoing, but first there was a sore trial for the little settlement to endure. In 870 the Danes came down on Dereham with fire and sword, leaving town and church in ashes, but even these blood-stained pagans did not violate Withburga's tomb. In the aftermath, the devastated Manor of East Dereham was bestowed on the Abbot of Ely in exchange for an undertaking to rebuild the church. It was a black day when the avaricious Abbot first set foot in the parish for he was quick to realise that in this small place was a treasure indeed to enrich his Abbey. He coveted the costly gifts laid at Withburga's shrine, and decided that she must be 'translated' to Ely [translation being, in this instance, a polite ecclesiastical term for stealing]. Plans were made accordingly; plans which one writer described as being made 'with a tact and precision that might have put the most accomplished London burglar to the blush'. Armstrong continues the story:

On the day appointed the Lord Abbot and some of the most active and prudent monks, attended by the sturdiest loaf-eaters of the abbey, all well armed, set out on their journey to steal the body of the saint; and on their arrival at Dereham they were received with great respect by the inhabitants. The Lord Abbot, as lord and proprietor, and chief-temporal as well as spiritual, held a court for the administration of justice. After this public court of justice the bountiful Lord Abbot bade the good people of Dereham to a feast. The whole day having been spent in feasting and drinking, and dark night coming on apace, the company retired by degrees, every man to his own house or hut.

It was then that this infamous Abbot, with his secret, black and midnight minions went, under cover of darkness, to the church and opened the tomb. Armstrong describes the robbery:

About the middle of the night, or between the third and fourth watch, when the matutina or lauds are begun to be sung, the coffin in which the body of the saint was inclosed, was put upon the shoulders of the active and prudent monks, who forthwith conveyed it in great haste, and without any noise— making to a wheeled car which had been provided for that purpose. The coffin was put into the car, the servants of the Abbot were placed as guards round about the car to defend it, the Lord Abbot and the monks followed the car in processional order, other well-armed loaf-eaters followed the Abbot and monks; and in this order they set forward for Brandon, and the banks of the river which leads towards the house of Ely. There they found ready and waiting for them the boats which the Abbot had commanded, and immediately embarking with their precious treasure, they hoisted all sail and made ply their oars at the same time.

In another version of these events is added the rather charming detail that 'they were accompanied during their whole journey thither by a very bright star which shone upon the virgin's body and emitted bright rays'.

Armstrong goes on to relate what happened when the theft was discovered:

Hullulu! never was such a noise heard in so small a place before. Every man, woman and child in Dereham was roused and ran shrieking to the empty tomb in the church, and at the sound of a horn, all the people from all the hamlets near unto the pleasant hill of Dereham came trooping in with bills and staves, not knowing what had happened but fancying that the fiery Dane had come again. But when they saw, or were told about the empty tomb, the people all shouted "Who hath done this deed? Who hath stolen the body of our saint?

Now no one could gainsay that the Abbot of Ely and his monks had done it. A serf who had gone early afield to cut the grass while the dew was on it, had met the car and the procession on the road between Dereham and Brandon ... and, so arming themselves with whatever weapons they could most readily meet with, they all poured out of Dereham and took the shortest way to Brandon. They were brisk men, these folk of the uplands, well exercised in the game of bowls and pitching the bar, and in running and leaping, and in wrestling on the church green; they were light-footed men, these men of Dereham; but although they ran their best, it was all too late when they got to Brandon, for the monks had got a long way down the river with the saint's body.

And so Withburga was borne away to her eternal exile in that grim place surrounded by impenetrable swamps like the dark land of Mordor where the Shadows lie. There she was interred with great pomp and ceremony alongside her sisters Etheldreda and Sexburga and her niece Ermenilda. During the service the astonished congregation saw once again evidence of her saintly incorruptibility:

Although she had been dead nearly 300 years the virgin princess with all her clothing was as fresh as ever and her limbs flexible, and so bashful was she at being looked at by the men, that when one of the monks ventured to touch her flesh a rosy blush suffused her cheeks.

Notwithstanding this Withburga appears to have been neglected at Ely where she only held the place of a younger sister, overshadowed by St Etheldreda, foundress of Ely Abbey and who, as the virgin wife of two husbands, was evidently herself a no mean miracle worker!

In course of time her tomb became dilapidated and the marble slab over it was fractured. The Abbey authorities did nothing about it and their negligence was reproved by finding the stone miraculously put together again, as entire and firm as if it had never been broken. What they ought to have done had been done for them by the saint herself.

Her last chronicled appearance was in 1169. A female in the habit of a nun appeared to a poor widow who was worshipping at the altar of St

Etheldreda, and told her she was Withburga and predicted the death of Nigellus, the then Bishop (somewhat gleefully, one suspects, since she had no cause to love the breed).

After that she was seen no more, and as a final indignity, the location of her tomb was eventually forgotten.

But Withburga was never forgotten in the town she had founded. On the site of her original tomb outside the church, as if in Divine recompense for our loss, a spring of lucid water had welled up, gifted with many healing virtues; and there it remains to this day, for not even the thieving monks of Ely could make off with a holy well. No doubt many a weary pilgrim padding along the hard and dusty road to Walsingham found rest and refreshment there. Indeed it became a place of pilgrimage in its own right with a Guild of St Withburga to minister to the pilgrims' needs.

But the healing reputation of the well lingered on long after that. William Cowper, who spent his last tormented years in these parts, sought solace there as described by George Borrow (one of our most famous sons) in the pages of *Lavengro*:

96 St Withburga's well.

> And no longer at early dawn does the sexton of the old church reverently doff his hat as, supported by some kind friend, the death-stricken creature totters along the church path to that mouldering edifice with the low roof, inclosing a spring of sanatory waters, built and devoted to some saint —if the legend over the door is true—by the daughter of an East Anglian king.

George's memory was at fault here, but then he was very young when he lived in Dereham.

Throughout the 19th century the well was tended with love and reverence. Parson Armstrong made this entry in his diary in 1860:

> My new parishioner, Miss Steele, is one of those delightful old maids you read of in novels. She has undertaken the garden of St. Withburga's Well, from which task she is good naturedly nicknamed after the Saint. It is wholesome and good to see the little woman working away until the 'ting tang' has ceased, and closing her labours with prayers in Church.

Today a commemorative service, with procession to the well, is held each year on or near 8 July, the date of the robbery. For the rest of the year we show our love and reverence by throwing discarded fish-and-chip wrappings and empty Coke cans into the water.

Meanwhile, poor lost Withburga rests somewhere beneath the canopy of Ely Cathedral ever pure and incorrupt; waiting for her star to rise again and light the way home to her beloved Dereham.

FRAGMENTS OF POEM
and
Extracts from Introductory Epistle.

"A DOLEFUL DISCOURSE and ruthfull Reporte of the great Spoyle and lamentable loss, by fire, in the Towne of East Dearham, in the Countie of NOR-FOLKE: Vpon Tuesday the 18 of Julie, this present yere 1581."

Hosea 5, verse 14, 15.
2 Cro. 36, verse 16.

"At London. Printed by Richard Bradocke, for Richarde Hollens: And are to be solde at his Shop ouer against the signe of the Bell within Algate. 1581."

"To my deare friende and christian Brother, Richard Atlee, Inhabitant of the desolate Towne of East dearham, and to his vertuous wife, Alice Atlee (1): Arthvr Gvrney wisheth prosperitie, and all good thinges, in Christ Jesv."

"About a fortnight since, it was my hap to understande of a Ballet (as I take it) then newly come from the Presse, conteyning a brief and doleful Discourse of the late burning of East DEREHAM. And (as for mine owne part) I both was and am a witnes of the wonderful euents therof: and there withall (what for my continuall tratell of body and mind, the ruines of my friendes and allies and mine owne smal losses) a fellow feeler of the heavy burthen imposed vpon the townes estate: euenso, with so much the more good will I enterteyned

(1) Richard Atlee and Alice Hempstead, married at Dereham, 3 Sep. 1564.

the newes, expecting some better sequell, and rested not, til mine eyes were testimonies of the trueth. But when I perused the same, and approued the penning as sufficient in that or such like cases, I was (neuerthelesse) well aduised of sundrie vntruthes, whiche the author (no doubt) not so much vppon pretenced deprauation, as for want of necessarie instruction had inserted. And albeit, no important thing hath therein escaped, which (for mine owne part) I would not tollerate, of verie good wil in that respect: yet sithe her Maiestie, her honorable counsaile, many noble, worshipful, and common personages, bee otherwise informed of the matter: as also, the duetie of a christien, requiring by all meanes to intercept the course of an vntrueth: and last of all, in diuersities of wandring reportes to establish some certaintie, I haue vndertaken in the discourse of the matter to sett downe such an assurance of his particuler errours, and in stead therof, interposed such trueth, as the diligent obseruation of mine owne experience and the triall of many sound iudgements can confirme and testifie.

¶ One poinct (therfore) wherin he failed, is touching the nomber of Tenementes, Messuages, or mansion houses subuerted and spoyled.

The 2. concerning the dissolution of our houses necessarie for diuers domestical vses.

¶ The 3. his insinuation of a totall losse and detriment susteined.

In these three (speciallie) hath he left the matter destitute of true report: for as I have expressed in the sequell of my treetise: the number of tenements is LII. whiche he calleth LX. The houses of office, 350. or there aboutes: which hee reducethe into the nomber of 80. The value of all together 8000 li, or very litle lesse, which he reporteth to be 14000. The two first (without al conttrouersie) are mistaken, and

Poem written in the 16th century and reproduced from Carthew's book of 1855, *History of East Dereham*.

78

published falselie : But as for the last, I must confesse, that (at a blush) it seemeth to carrie great appearance of trueth : and I my selfe was therin greatly oueroeene & deceiued, vntil with certaine other (of good experience) I had made an estimate of euerye particuler losse, and brought them to a generall and grosse summe.

Neuerthelesse, if we may recken the charge, which the towne (if ever she be repayred) wil exact, to make returne of her former estate, I meane in number and quantitie of houses, and (therwith) not pretermit her manifold losses, namely of coyne, corne, implements of Householdstuffe, victuales, wood, Timber, chattell, fruict, wels, pumps, hay, straw, time and trades, wherby ever since they have declined and gone backward, which with the rest are or ought to be brought into the rekning : It is certaine true, that of, 14000 li. a small remnant wyll remaine, if any deale be left at all.

A. 2.

But this is an other case : for an accompt is rather to be raised accordinge to the rate of so much money as euery mans house and stuffe would yeald in sale, if now it weare in STATV QVO PRIVS. For albeit the buildinges were such as might have serued many yeares and ages, if it had pleased the Lorde to permitte them to posteryties : yet of a newe house, in quantitie of proportionable resemblance with an old, and of an old, is not one and the selfe same reason : because by how mvch it exceedeth in goodnes, by so mvch ought it to be preferred in price and estimation.

So then the whole losse which the towne hath susteyned is 8000 li, or there abouts, & the reedifying or restauration of the same in necessarie maner with such other reconings adherent as I have allready cast ouer, will then amount to litle lesse then 14000, and so it seemeth not vainely saide

He that buyeth a house ready wrought,
Getteth many a nayle for nought.

79

Thus much Sir, touching the cause that moued me to intermedle & busie my selfe about the affayres of this processe."

I have extracted thus much of Arthur Gurney's prefatory letter, verbatim, partly as a specimen of his style of prose composition for comparison with the poem following, and partly because it will be seen that the numbers of dwelling-houses and out-houses, mentioned in the poem(3), correspond with those stated by the Epistle to have been burnt: therefore this production is distinguished from the ballad upon the same subject, previously printed, the mis-statements in which he undertakes to correct. And from these premises, I draw the conclusion, that the Poem itself, was the composition of Arthur Gurney.

He proceeds to point out that "the Lord, of his owne "especiall grace, from amongest the rest of that part of the "towne destroyed," had gleaned out Mr Atlee's house, "as one "eare out of a shocke of corne, and preserued it alone amids "the multitude of so monsterous flames." And he argues, at great length, against those who would rather ascribe the fire itself, and the circumstances attending it, and its final extinction, to natural causes, than to the Divine Providence. He deplores the folly and blindnesse of such persons, and tells them that "they might gather a heape of myracles together, "passed in the ruines of this our towne, and by the same "learne to knowe the prouidence of God." These I shall quote. .

"As the wall couered with drye & parched strawe, which

(3) While these pages were passing through the Press, my attention was directed to a Catalogue of Mr Thorpe, the Bookseller, offering for sale, another sheet of this "excessively rare poem," which he ascribed, merely from its style of language, to Churchyard. I secured the purchase of the fragment, consisting of eight mutilated pages, which are reprinted in those followvtg.

80

although it be platted where the fire had free accesse and stood like a stake in the midest of ouerwhelming floudes, yet doth it stand whole and sound, yea &, which is more, with one of the corner postes burnt a good depth iust in the midst of the top, with strawes stroughtinge ouer it vnperished. What? hath fortune care of strawes? or could these (little wretches) laye hold on her heary side, & a whole streat of houses so many furlongs long not misse the bald. Oh fine strawes, if your dexteritie have saued you, thanke your selves. If Fortune, fie on her harlot, that would be so freendly vnto you, who neuer did her good, and so froward to the rest, that neuer wisht her harme.

Lykewise the winde which allwayes changed in defence of those houses that nowe stand, and then were in danger, may shew how farr the Lord did purpose to reache his rod. It cannot be denied with anye colloure of trueth, that when the fire had gotten the market stead, the wind from the sowthwest chaunced full west, whereby that side was pre-serued, and when it had gotte, by your house and beyond it, so that had the fire taken the next rowe, the remnant, except God being able to do what he wil, had shewed a wonderful myracle: must of necessitie haue gon with the fore end of the pece, then I say he brought the winde from the west to the northwest, which kept off both the blaze & sparcks & turned them almost backe again, or at the least, that way wherin lay no danger. If any deny this, not only my selfe who duly obsuered these alterations as I labored, but other credible witnesses also can testifie with me, & in the end when the fire was suppressed & beaten downe, then lo, it returned into the same stead wherin it stode at the first.
A. 3.

Moreouer, why cannot our fortune men gather nothing out of the preseruation of your house knowing that an other

81

was burnt to the earth, which in the on end, namli on the street syde was ioyned to it and came somewhat within it and on the back syde betwene the foundations of the crosse buildings was at the most but foure foot distance, so that by al likelihood of imagination the enes of ech other must concur within lesse then thre quarters of a yard? if thei say your mansion hous (wherof the question is) is a tiled house & that you had the assistance of the pit & great help of mans hand, I graunt. But I pray you who put that boldnes and courage in one only man, whom we neuer before knew desperat in rash attempts when your hous was al redy fired, for want of ladders to break out between two spars, there to indure that great peril & danger that not only his parents & frends cried out on, but al the standers by also for dread of his present death? who I say in this notable distres made him the instrument of your good & an incoragement to the rest? was it God or fortune? now, al this say our Epicures was fortune forsoth: it was but good & euill luck, it was but habardepas, it was but this or that, & which for a penny. Alas if I should go about to persuade them that before the pit was made, or er the hous was raised, or er your were born, God held the purpose of your defence, I think thei would iudge me mad, and yet it is greater madnes by oddes to denye it.

Finallie in a world of such witnesses & arguments of the prouidence of God to make short with them & conclude in a word: so sone as the fire was ceased, who sent that notable shoure of rain? was it fortune to show herself in her pontificalibus, or the Lord to declare to vs & proue what he cold haue don in time for our safty, if it pleased him? they which ascribe these things to fortune, let them set her on the top of the pinacle, rest in her contemplation

I

82

& seruice & seek non other gods, for she is euen good ynough to show them experience of eternall shame."

He concludes this quaint epistle by exhorting his friends at least to derive a practical lesson from that evidence of God's love to them, "and as you have hitherto been countenancers of the poore professors of Jesus Christ in this your town, and louing friends to al other, so herafter be not wanting (as I trust you wil not) in reforming and bridling those whose religion and maners you daily see too far out of square and order, &c."

"Yours, in the Lord,
AR. GURNEY."

NOTE.

The nine verses immediately following are printed on the same sheet as this letter. The sheet obtained from Mr Thorpe having been mutilated at the bottom, some of the verses in that portion of the poem are imperfect. The type of the verses in the original is in black letter, otherwise they are reprinted almost literatim.

83

A LAMENTABLE DISCOURSE OF THE SPOYLE OF

EAST DEARHAM.

Who markes the steps of thys unstayed state,
And sees the seas which sink vs in our sin,
And wiseli weies our wicked wandring gate,
And floudes of filth that we lye frozen in,
Maye mourne with me, our cases are akinne.
I tyed my trust to trifling trash and pelfe,
He by my harme maye seeke to saue himselfe.

Least they be reserued for as great or greater iudgement.

A Towne I was though blest, not brave, God wott,
Ne of renoune, my name was allwayes small,
My treasures thinne, yet trades which I had gott,
Did hould me high uppon an happy stall:
An ayde was I, but in no case a thrall,
To neighbour Townes dispersed heare and there,
My state was sound and stoode for stately chere.

A Towne of meane report.

My fields full faire, my pastures pight for good,
My waters cleare, my fruict sufficient:
My bounds both broade and well bestad with wood,
My comons large and comly to content:
But oh, my sinne deserued to be shent,
And lowde did call the vengeance of my God,
Who heard at last, and lasht mee with his Rod.

Comodyties

84

For lo, where late I was a Towne at needes,
Where Iudgementes and where lawes were oft
   discust,
Am now become a nettle bush of weedes,
Defaste with fire and halfe returnd to dust :
My name to ken, who so hath any lust,
   Dearham I am, scituate next the East,
   In *Norfolk* soile, full well for man and beast.

[margin: East Dearham.]

Come foorth, therfore, both friend and foe, I meane,
I counsell all, and none would ouerpasse :
Come learne of mee, that whylome sounde did
   dreame
Of happy state, but saw not what it was,
A world of sinnes hath caused my disgrace :
   Yea, comon faultes, and in no calme degree,
   Therfore, I say, now see your selues by mee.

[margin: Meaning all other townes and warnyng them.]

When as I stoode in peace and pleasant rest,
Guarded with these and pleasures many moe :
My pleasant pathes so promist mee the best,
That (voide of dread) I doubted no such bloe :
For why? the tempest that hath wrought my woe,
   Was out of sight and couerd with a clowde,
   Which causd mee pranck, oh wretch and
      patern prowde.

Why should I count, the courses of my cryme?
Syth true it is, I plunged was most deepe
In eche offence that doth reproch the tyme,
And in these daies so rocke the worlde asleep?
My sinnes, my sinnes, have caused mee to weepe,
   Whome God hath made a myrour to them all,
   That see my sore, or euer serch it shall.

85

A Drunkard (friends) was I with deepe delight,
And pamperd vp my paunche with belly cheere ;
I left not so, but styll came on foorthright,
To thousandes moe, than I haue cited heere :
I cared not to cogge, to lye and sweare,
   To boast and brawle, I thought no simple sport,
   Ne yet the good, with spite to misreport.

[margin: Drunken-nes goeth not alone.]

Thus, by degrees, I practised my parte,
For (whirlyng now) come Whordome on withall,
Selfewyll, Hatred, and swellyng Pride of hart,
The lacke of Loue, did throughly make mee thrall :
I serued myselfe, and poasted next the wall
   My neighbour, friend or foe, what ere he was,
   As though I raued, to ride on *Mydas* Asse.

[Here is an hiatus of a whole sheet containing eight pages
or forty-eight verses ; those which follow are reprinted from
Mr Thorpe's sheet.]

Loe friends you see the cause of all my wrecks,
Euen sinne it was that stroocke this fearefull stroake,
Nowe shall you heare the forme of such effects,
As do pursue them which the Lord prouoke,
Theyr glory fades and falles away like smoke,
   Expert am I and witnesse in the case,
   Whose fumeing faults haue thus besmeard my
      face.

[margin: Cause.]

[margin: Effects.]

Attend therefore the sequell of my tale,
And I shall showe the shape of my myshapp,
Beleeue me well I will not passe my pale,
But truely touch the trueth in euery gapp,
For why? to hull or luske in lyers lapp,
   Ought duely of all men to be abhorde,
   Nowe lyst I say, and do the trueth recorde.

86

When *Loue* my iudge the mighty Lord on highe,
Had looked long and could not see me come,
And when I card not for his call and crye,
Ne would bestirde to stoupe vnto his doome,
And when I showde my selfe both deaf and dum,
Then up he starts and straight had pight the plott
Which staind my state, and layd me to my lott.

Without recovery.

For at the least, more than a monthe right out,
Before he blew the brand that burnt me thus,
He sent a season of sunneshyne and drowght,
No day came downe to dewe my vtter......
But parcht me like the perfect tynder......
So that the steele no sooner gaue the stroake,
Bnt flames flew out and ...ded unto smoake.

Drowght,

*

The time of yeare, was br.... to the touche,
For Julie did her drie daies beginne,
Who to the matche the candle well could couche,

This spoken, tautum secunduum.

*

(*Desunt four lines.*)

The eighteenth day of that same mournfull moone,
Within the year of thincarnation
Of Christ our Lord Gods welbeloued sonne,
One thousand fiue hundreth eightie and one.
Before eleuen a clocke in the forenoone,
I tooke my course into *Ecliptica,*
And leaft my lampe in lewde *Saturnica.*

IVLY.

A comparison borrowed of the Moone entring into the line of eclipp.

87

For why, the Lord did hide him nowe behinde,
The center of his whole consuming yre,
And now my sinne the torture so vnkinde,
Opposde me iust wherof arouse the fire,
For loke howe much my flames encreased hier,
So much they dimd and daunted my estate,
And causd me crouch vnto a crabbed fate.

My streets were longest twixt the South and North,
And therin peard such beauty as I bare,
My breadth from East to West did passe right forth,
And as in townes crosse streets full comon are,
Right so in me they went and planted were.
Whereby fower wayes the fier soone was spred,
All which at one must needes annoye my head.

The situation of the towne.

The winde (God wot) did waite at the southwest,
To blowe the blaze into the market plot,
All things were armd and redy to arrest,
My careles corps, that all mishaps forgot,
Wherefore I serued am, full lyke a sot,
For lo, euen in the midst of the high streate,
The euilles we....n which did me thus intreate.

He al..eth stil vn...n eclipps.

The winde.

* * *

As for the man with whom it first begyn,
The heauens behold I would not h..e his cryme,
Yet I suppose he hath committed sinne
Which lately gald him ....hlesse rime.

Where the fire beganne.

* * *
* *
(*Desunt three lines.*)

88

He is (no doubt) a sinner with the rest,
And beares the Badge of *Adames* beastly parte,
And broodes the bale, that breedes within his brest,
And hoordes the harmes that hanges on eche mans hart,
I know what I could say of his desart,
But let that passe, I am not here to tell
Of praise, but how with mee it late befell.

Betwixt the wife and maide of that same man,
Right true it is, my bane at first brake out,
To whome (lykewise) no harme adiuge I can,
In this their fact, for why? what man can doubt,
But that they rued the ruine of this route?
Besides (my frendes) in all these flames and smoake,
We may be sure, the Lorde did strike his stroake.

This being thus, why should I chalke his chaunce?
With markes of mallice and of fowle despight,
Full well I see, he did but leade the Daunce :
For many moe were pesterd in that plight,
Yet all (I deeme) with verie dull delight :
1 Pet.4,17. And sith I knowe, God eft with his beginnes,
Why do I poinct at this man and his sinnes?

Admit the Lorde would wrest from him my woe,
And first of all, put him in for his parte,
Shall I anone, my wayes and wantes let goe,
As though my selfe had neare deseru'd to smarte,
None can so compt, but being fond in hart,
Let me (therfore) still as I ought beleeue,
That he hath tane, which first to me did geeue.

89

But nowe egaine, I turne me to my tale,
My Belles were ronge, and I straight waies aroase,
My neighbours heard them both from Hill and dale.

*   *   *
*   *   *

(*Desunt four lines.*)

Yet sith I say, I could not vnderstand,
Ne search the secretes of his holy head,
Nor see how farre he would stretch foorth his hand, Means vsed
Nor what for mee he had afore decreed :
I left no let that might mee stand in stead,
But used those my Masteries in chiefe,
That promist most, yet least did ease my griefe.

Some water drewe, some did the same transporte,
Some Ladders reard and ran to houses toppes,
Some spread wet cloathes, and some in wofull sorte,
Came headlong downe from Eues where water drops,
Some counsaile gaue, and called other fops,
Some cride allowde, do reare before the fire,
And some bad rend, but where I woud repair.

Some sought to saue some lynnen cloth and ware,
And some againe my coyne gan fast convay,
Some came with Carts, and with whole loades of care
Some Goodes did leade into the fields and way,
Some for their deedes and Euidences pray,
Some. that were stoarde of vittailes and of graine,
Did see it burne vnto their losse and paine.

K

94

Alas the while, what sight was this to see,
I got a bed, the fier gainde a house,
I chopt a chip, it tooke away the tree :
    *   *   *   *
    (*Desunt four lines.*)

.. rey in.

For after it had once begonne to fume,
Against the winde, and with the winde it went,
It leaft no side, but eftsoones did assume,
All that it toutcht, and no way would be pent,
Till my long streetes, on both sides it had brent,
    And made them lowe and leauell with the grownde,
    And of my coyne, had molten many a pownde.

.: vme
.: ses.

The Houses Mansion, which it brought downe,
Were fiftie-two, euen there aboutes I gesse,
And all the rest, that burnt were in the Towne,
Three hundred and fiftie, not many moe ne lesse,
So that the totall number I confesse,
    Is foure hundred and twaine which I clearly lost,
    And now do lacke, to my great griefe and cost,

The Fish and flesh, that I forehande preparde,
The Drinke, the drugges, the bread, butter and cheese,

... ke.

The Hay, the strawe, the wood for whiche I carde,
All at a clappe, I must forgoe and leese :
The Catchpole caught them as his lawfull fees,
    Which laide me supperlesse vpon my Bed,
    When I scarce fownde a cowch to calme my head.

95

The Fruict that late I looued to pare and prune,
I nowe could reache well roasted from the trees,
Hunger with care, had harpt so sweete a tune,
That Bisket Boxes, Carrawayes, and these,
I leaft at large, for daintie waspes and Bees,
    And now could leape alofte to catch a crust,
    And snap it up with Appetite and lust.

. . er is a
sause.

And doubtlesse, who had heard the Infantes moane,
For lacke of lodging and accustomed fare,
Or of the ...... and burnt, the grieuous groane,
    *   *   *   *
    (*caetera desunt.*)

.. moane.

90

Some from the field returned soone and fast,
But were shut out, and could no where get in,
Some to scape out, with baggage ran in haste,
And could perceiue no fawte where to begin,
Thus some and some great wearinesse did winne,
Untyll the some was verie scant and small,
That idle stoode, and in no stead at all.

And what for this? where is the gaine I got?
My meanes did fade, and fall flat to the grounde,
And all my helpes and handes were staid (God wott)
        *   *   *
        *   *   *
    (Desunt four lines.)

Ladders
burnt.

For loe, the Ladders that were soone set up,
The fier did force to fall right downe as fast:
My strength was staid, that I mought sup the Cup,
And ken my selfe a captiue at the last,
The winde did ware, as though it made great haste,
    To fling the flames of foule fate aboute,
    And could reioyce my weale to scorne and flowt.

Benefite of
water lost.

And where my aide in water chiefly lay,
As in a meane for suche distresse preparde,
And where I made my most recourse that way,
My footing fayld till all my Mart was mard,
Full sodenly therof was I debard:
    For why? the brandes, they whirld so fast
       aboute,
    They burnt my Pumps, I wor my welles right
       out.

91

And where my wares was poasted too and fro,
And leaft at large, for euery man to see,
Fewe bought (God knowes) but many borrowed so, Pylferers.
That I haue cause to curse their knauerie:
And shall no lesse, (I doubt mee) while I die:
    For though euyll windes do blowe some men
       to good,
    Yet are they lewde, that liues by others foode.

Nay, lowdly lewde, and most accursed wightes,
Be they who see the Thunderboultes of God,
Aboute their cares, and still dare vse the sleightes, The
wickednes
of men.
And in their theft and villanie thus plod,
Where shall they haue their lasting place and boade,
    In heauen? no, here I pawne and pledge my soule,
    Except they turne, and tame suche fancies
       fowle.

Can any beast that feede on carren vile?
Or can the Dogge spew out suche filth as this?
Or can the Deuyll more damnably beguile?
        *   *   *   *
        *   *   *   *
    (Desunt four lines.)

If Pallas had set ouer all her skill,
Or were my tongues more then were Argus eyes,
Or had I got the trade of Tullies Quill:
These often tould, could me not halfe suffice,
To paint and portray out in worthy wise,
    The sore, the sinne, the shamefull partes of man:
    Whose mind and moode no meane but madnes
       can.

92

Natural causes.

For though the Lorde imprints in clowde and skie,
Right strange Edictes, to call us home from sinne,
And so by signes of Iudgementes dayly trie,
The canckred case that we lie tumbling in,
Yet nothing wyll our wandring sences winne,
We straight, in nature, can discerne the cause,
And so ascribe eche thing vnto her lawes.

We diuerslie can descant of the Earth,
And dull us in our deep deuices so,
And showe the cause of plentie and of dearth,
And what doth shake the grounde, and manie moe,
We are so farre betwitcht and gone in woe,
Than when the Lord doth plead our plagues by word,
We shift it off, as though he did but bourd.

Doubtlesse I deeme, or (rather see right well)
That if from Heauen, we heard his voice and crie:
Or if he sent the seelie soules from Hell:

Dives and Lazarus.

To warne vs by their wofull miserie,
We would accompt all this but fablerie,
So that (alas) I can not iudge ne thinke,
What may us saue, that haue such mindes to sincke.

Nature.

If fearefull Comete glide ouer our head,
Or blasing Starres shine in our shameles eyes,
If Sicknesse haue our sore both brought and bred,

* * * *
(*Desunt four lines.*)

93

Few prooffes herein may seeme sufficient,
For (out alas) how many way the trueth,
Myne eyes, myne eyes, want no experiment,
That may me driue to dole and double ruthe,
For of my heauy harmefull hap ensuthe,
Nought els with most, but discord and disdaine,
And of my losse, haue many made their gaine.

But if they feare the iudgements of the Lord,
Or knewe from whence this passing plague did springe,
Or would not wrongly still my case recorde,
Ne shrowd my shame vnder their fortunes winge,
They would be carefull of this cruell thinge,
And rather learne to leaue for fear of paine,
Than loue so long to liue by trayters traine.

But all in vaine I seeme thus to inuey,
Their frozen heartes I feare not soone can thowe,
They haue ben taught and truely told the waye,
How they might gaine, and in God's fauour growe,
But they are deafe, they loue to heare of snowe,
Therefore I leaue them that will filthy bee,
And so againe vnto my tale do flee.

When as I sawe I was so sore beset,
On ery side, that now no hope I had,
And that my meanes did fall into the net,
And all was fishe that came, bothe good and bad,
Right hastily and all, in care yclad,
I muckehild vp, my mooueables and stuffe,
And shortely saued myckle mangled shruffe.

No . . .

The p . . . . .
after th . . .
in feart . . .
ner, ch . . .
to rest . . .
the stol . . .

Appendix III

Letter from Rev. Charles Hyde Wollaston, 22 Jan. 1834 (See p. 68)

TO THE PARISHIONERS
OF THE
PARISH OF EAST DEREHAM, NORFOLK.

After a residence of twenty five years, during which time the greatest harmony has generally prevailed amongst us, I am concerned to find that the same horrid spirit of factious discontent, which has produced so much mischief in other places, has at length appeared here, and made great inroads on the peace of this hitherto quiet Parish. Till of late the Churchwardens and myself have possessed (as I may boldly say we deserve) the confidence of the Parish at large, and we may defy any one to shew an instance in which that confidence has been intentionally abused.

I am grieved to say that recently there has arisen a factious party amongst us, who make it their sole business to excite ill will, and attend Parish Meetings for the express purpose of finding fault with the customs of this hitherto peaceful place; and, through the negligence of the well disposed there is a set crept in amongst us, who, by their *united* and *persevering* efforts, are fast obtaining the entire dominion and final destruction of every comfort in the parish.

The first step of those open enemies and their short-sighted abettors, was to procure the choice of Overseers, who are never to be seen at Church; but whether they had previously shewn any other proofs of their deserving the confidence of the Inhabitants, I am at a loss to determine. The manner however in which they have executed their office, the means by which the oppressed have been deprived of any benefit from that appeal, which in other places is a check upon the measures of Overseers; and the insolent language which they and their abettors have addressed to men of unquestionable respectability, are as well known as they are generally reprobated. But besides the conduct of the present Overseers in the discharge of the duties belonging to their office, it ought to be generally known (as I am sure it will be generally felt and resented) that they, for the first time, have taken upon themselves to interfere with the highly respectable Churchwardens in the execution of their office; and, having actually refused to pay for the Sacramental Bread and Wine which has been provided for your use, these same Overseers are now threatening to obtain a Mandamus from the Court of King's Bench, to compel the Churchwardens to proceed to the election of an Organist, without proper time for consideration; a matter which, as none of the present Overseers ever attend Church, must (unless indeed they have some other secret view) be perfectly unimportant to them as individuals, and with which, as the Salary is not paid by Rate at all, they can have as little business to interfere, as our

Churchwardens would have to dictate who should hold the office of Sexton or Pew-opener at the Independent Meeting-house. Be assured however that it is not the filling up of this paltry place, (which ought to rest with the members of the Church) at which this party are aiming; but this step is neither more nor less than a covert attack upon the very existence of the Church itself, made by the Dissenters under the sanction and with the co-operation of those who ought to know better. I cannot for the moment suppose these proceedings arise from the ill will of sensible or respectable persons against myself as an individual, because I am not conscious of having merited it. I know however, that as the head of the Church here, and as having always supported poverty against oppression, and the upright against the dishonest and unprincipled, I must necessarily incur hostilities. These commotions amongst us must decidedly originate in the malevolence of a party, who are endeavouring with too much success throughout the Kingdom to degrade the Church, and render it contemptible as a preparatory step to its *final overthrow*. I am not unjust enough to attribute such conduct to a *majority*, or even to any considerable number of my Parishioners, but unfortunately most of the respectable Inhabitants, too inconsiderately concluding that a few right-minded persons who attend the Vestries are able to transact the business without their presence, absent themselves from Parish Meetings, because they are unwilling to put themselves in the way of hearing the abusive and insulting language of our enemies.

It is under these circumstances that I feel myself called upon to remind you all that you have a duty to perform to *yourselves* , to *the Poor*, to me as your Clergyman, and to the Church of which you are the firm and conscientious Members. You must know that the Churchwardens cannot resist the torrent which is ready to overwhelm you without your presence; neither can I continue to preside at your Vestry Meetings, as I have always made a point of doing for the benefit of the Parish for so many years, unless I have the whole support of those who are members of the Church. Indeed, I cannot condescend to sit there surrounded by your enemies as I have lately done without your united support. You must be aware that these things are perfectly unimportant to me as an individual, and that I should greatly promote my own personal ease and comfort by declining all interference in parochial concerns. This, however, I am unwilling to do, so long as I see any prospect of your co-operation and support in upholding your rights and privileges, but unless you afford me and the Churchwardens your countenance at every Vestry, I must, (however unwillingly) adopt this line of conduct and leave the management of your affairs in the hands of your bitterest foes.

I feel that I have a personal claim upon your attendance, and unless you wish your *Poor* to be oppressed, your *Church* to be degraded, its *Officers* to be insulted, and your *Pews* to be occupied by Dissenters, you must attend the Vestries; you must chose a *majority at least* of Parish Officers from the Members of the Church, and you must support your Minister and Churchwardens in what they know to be essential for the preservation of your rights and privileges.

I call upon you then, the firm and conscientious *Members of the Church,* I call upon you as *Friends of the Poor,* I call upon you as *the Enemies of discord,* and I call upon you as persons *educated under my own eye,* to come boldly forward and support your own cause, and maintain the religious establishment of your forefathers, and if after this appeal, you fail to support us the Minister and Churchwardens, I shall satisfy myself that I have discharged my duty by thus attempting to rouse you from your lethargy, and although I forsee the fatal consequences to the Parish I must leave you to the dominion of a restless faction, whom you are too idle to resist, and must give up the pleasure I have hitherto derived from the unanimity of my assembled parishioners.

That you may now see your danger, and with one mind and one voice shew the power you possess to frustrate the designs of open enemies and insiduous friends, is the fervent prayer of

Your devoted Servant,

CHARLES HYDE WOLLASTON.

East Dereham.
January 22, 1834.

Appendix IV

The Dereham Survey, continued from p. 8

The demesne of the manor is thus viz—in the field which is called Toppeswellwong 7½a. In Milnewong 10a. In Voellewong 7a. In Gallestoft 6a 1r. Behind the mesuage of Henry the Vintner 4½a and 1a. In Hilwong 11½a. In Hilgate 1a and 3r. In Netherwenestoft 16a. In Overweneshiltoft 10a. In Rodewong 14a. In Abelmerewong 8½a. In Chyretrewong 9a. At Byhotemerewong 16a. In Medwescote 5a 1r. In Scorelond without the park 13a. In Fiscpet without the park 27a. In Stabbilond of (de) the park 29½a. At the park gate 9a. In Gosewong 21a. Without the walls of the market 8½a. In Elnynestoft 6a 1r. In Croswong 19½a. In the other Crossewong 18a. In Overcrosswong 18a. In Qualmstowewong 19½a. In Nolling 14a 1r. In Tothil 6½a

The sum of the whole cultivated land is 358½a by the little hundred and by the perch of 16½ft which can be tilled by two ploughs—that is to say, of four oxen and two stots apiece—by the boon and customary works of the town. Moreover there are two horses there for carrying and harrowing. And be it known that each acre is worth 12d per annum by the extent as the jurors say.

The sum of that extent per annum is £17 18s. 6d.

Next, the Pastures and commons are detailed:

Of the meadow for the mowing viz. By Toppeswell, behind the grange of the manor 1a 3r by the said perch, which are worth per annum 4s.

Of the several pasture viz. In Bromlond below the park 25½a. In Medwescot below the park 11½a. In Cowesik 3a 3r. Sum of the whole several pasture 40a 3r by the said perch, whereof each acre extends to 10d per annum. Item, there is there a certain other several pasture which is called Ressemor and it cannot be measured on account of the water, which is worth per annum 2/6d. Item, the extent of several pastures per annum 36s 5½d.

Of the turbary. To the same manor belongs a certain turbary which is called Etlingeker which contains by 1 leuca in length by estimation viz. from Wodewell as far as Thokesfailyate and in breadth from the street which is called Kergate as far as a water course. In which turbary the whole soke of Derham of the Bishop's homage and the towns of Jakesham, Mateshale, Tudenham ought to common with the Lord Bishop, horn under horn with their beasts only, but not to cut wood nor to dig turves without the Bishop's licence. And in the same way the Lord Bishop with all his town ought to common in the turbary of the aforesaid towns on the other side of the stream with their beasts only, like as they with them. And in the same way in Tudenham Ker as far as Tudenham Faylyate and thence as far as Benjamin's house and the Faylyate of Becstede.

Item, to the same belongs a certain other turbary which is called Brunesmor which begins at Haweford and continues to Westfeldbek, viz by half a leuca by estimation, and in breadth by two furlongs and elsewhere in places by one furlong. In which turbary the whole town of Dereham and the homages of William de Bello Monte in Little Derham and of Gilbert de Fransham in

Skerning and of William de Stuteville in Grassehale ought to common with the Lord Bishop horn under horn with their beasts only but not to cut wood nor to dig turves without the lord's licence. And in the same way the Lord Bishop and all that his town of Derham ought to common with the aforesaidtowns of Derham amd Skerning, horn under horn, like as they with them. Item, to the same belongs a certain other turbary which is called Rokemede, which stretches in length from the mesuage of William de Insula as far as the mesuage of Ralph Ringerose, viz, by half a leuca by estimation. And in breadth by half a leuca in the middle, and elsewhere in places by one furlong where the town of Derham and the homage of William de Stukewile in Grassenhale, and the homage of Gilbert de Franshem in Scerning and the homage of William de Bello Monte in Little Derham ought to common with the Lord Bishop by feeding with their beasts horn under horn only; but not by digging turves except to the use of the Bishop. And in the same way the Lord Bishop and all that his town ought to common with the aforesaid towns on the other side of the stream in their turbary with their beasts only horn under horn.

Item, to the same belongs a certain common pasture which is called Galewerremor where all that town ought to common with the Lord Bishop by feeding horn under horn with their beasts only, but not by digging turves except by the licence of the lord. And it stretches in length by three furlongs by estimation and in breadth by two furlongs. Item, to the same belongs a certain other common pasture which is called Nortphalegrene which stretches in length by half a leuca by estimation and in breadth by one furlong where all that town and thirteen of the homage of William de Stuteville and Thomas de Hereford dwelling by that pasture ought to common with the Lord Bishop with their beasts horn under horn. Item, to the same belongs a certain other common pasture which is called Etlingegrene which stretches in length and breadth, viz—each way, by one furlong by estimation where all that town and the towns of Jakesham, Mateshale and Tudenham ought to common with the Lord Bishop with their beasts, horn under horn. Item, to the same belongs a certain other common pasture which is called Moregategrene which stretches in length by two furlongs by estimation and in breadth by one furlong, where all this town and the homage of William de Bello Monte in Little Derham and of William de Stuteville and Gilbert de Fransham in Skerning ought to common with the Lord Bishop with their beasts horn under horn and in the same way the Lord Bishop and all this town ought to common with them in their pasture in Berkestehall, horn under horn, like as they with them. And to the same belongs a certain other common pasture which is called Southwodegrene which continues in length by one furlong and a half by estimation and in breadth by six perches where all this town and the towns of Jakesham, Mateshale and Tudenham ought to common with the Lord Bishop with their beasts only horn under horn, but not to cut wood or to dig turves. Item, to the same belongs a certain other common pasture in the hamlet of Ho which is called Apelho and Lymcroft, which contains in length by half a leuca by estimation, and in breadth by a furlong where the homage of the Bishop and William de Stukewill of Ho and Thomas de Hereford ought to common with the Bishop with their beasts horn under horn. And be it known that all the aforesaid turbaries are worth per annum to the Lord Bishop 10li, sometimes more, sometimes less. And be it known that all the tenants of the Bishop in this town of Dereham ought to common with their beasts in the fields and lands of the lord after the corn has been carried, except the assart lands by the park towards the north, and so from day to day up to the Purification of the Blessed Mary, but the lords beasts shall first enter. And for having this commonage they shall yearly plough a certain arable tilth (arura) which is called Graserthe as appears below, but from the Purification of the Blessed Mary until the harvest no one shall enter the said fields nor lands with his beasts without the lord's license. And that several pasture is worth per annum 20s 6d sometimes more, sometimes less.

Then follows a record of the woods, fisheries, mills etc.

There is a wood which is called The Park which contains in itself six score and ten acres by estimation: whereof the underwood is worth per annum 30s and the pasturage 30s and the fern 15s. Sum 75s.

There is there one other wood which is called Toftwode which contains in itself five score acres by estimation: where the underwood is worth per annum 16s and sometimes more and the fern 3s. Sum 19s.

And be it known that the lord has his free warren in all this manor, both in the woods, lands, meadows and pastures and in the commons and turbaries.

Of the Fisheries belonging to the same, viz - The New Pool at Estmelne where no one ought to fish except only the Bishop. And likewise the pool of Kirkemelne, which is the Bishop's several fishery. Item, the jurors say that Bishops John and Geoffrey and their predecessors fished in the pool of Belhusmilne by right but the lady of Belhus now witholds that fishery from the Bishop's Bailiffs.

There are there three mills of which two are watermills and one a windmill: and the jurors say that there could be another windmill there at the lord's convenience, if he wished. And that the said three mills are worth per annum 10 marks.

There is there a market which is worth per annum 10 marks, as the jurors say.

Item, of stock, there can be there ten cows and one free bull: Thirty pigs and one free boar: Two hundred sheep by the greater hundred.

At this point the Bishop's tenants are brought into the picture. They are detailed under 10 headings:

Of Knights. Free Tenants. Customers and Farmers. Of Jakesham. Workers holding full lands. Workers holding half full lands. Workers holding 6 acres of land. Those holding 4 acres of land. Those new enfeofed. Of the Market.

The only entry under the first heading 'Of Knights' reads:

The Lady Alina la Marschale holds in Hokeringe with appurtenances a fee of three knights by knights service.

There were 34 free tenants, the entry in respect of the largest holding reads:

Hugh de Camera and Isabel his wife hold 200 acs of land for 18s 1d per annum equably. And they ought to fence 24 perches round the Bishop's park and 24 perches round Toftwode without food every year when there is need, but that he shall have the old hedge. And the perch shall be 20ft in length. And they owe suit of court and one suit of the hundred yearly.

Next come 'Customers and Farmers'. These tenants had far more onerous duties to perform, as the entry for Nicholas, son of Walter, who held four acres for 13d and had a one-eighth share in a further 10 acres shows:

Nicholas, the son of Walter, holds 4a for 13d equably. And he shall plough 1½a of custom at the lord's food as the others. And he shall come with as many as he yokes to one boon work of the ploughs at the lord's food, and if he has not an ox then he shall work that day from morning up to the unyoking of the ploughs at the ordering of the bailiff at the lord's food in the same manner. And he shall find a man, reaping at the lord's food, at each of the 3 boon works in harvest: And similarly a man at the fourth boon work, which is called 'lovebene', at the lord's food. And on every coming of the lord he ought to cut wood or to make faggots from morning up to the none (noon) hour without food. And he shall watch (for) robbers according to the turn of his neighbours without food. And he gives a hen at Christmas and 2 eggs and a half at Easter. And he shall give pannage for his swine if he has them as the others. And he shall give tallage at the lord's will. His sheep shall not lie in the lord's fold nor shall he give foldage: but he shall give childwit and fine for his daughters at the lord's will. And if he dies, then his heir shall make fine with the lord for relief as best he can.

Item, the same Nicholas, son of Walter, and William le Meillus, John son of Eufemia and Stephen de Elmam, Roger at Dam, Ralph le Cupere, Henry le Wyneter, Ralph de Humbletoft hold 10a which were Ralph's, son of Henry, for 3s 4d equably. And they give a hen and 5 eggs, And they shall fence 8 perches round the park and have the old hedge: And they shall plough 1 acre with food: And they owe two foot journeys per annum, to Norwich or Lynn or elsewhere to similar places within the waters without food, and the other customs as the same Nicholas for his other tenement above, but if he does not make those two journeys, then he shall give for each 1½d only.

There are 146 names listed under this heading. Most of the duties detailed end with 'and perform other customs as the aforesaid Nicholas'.

Under the heading of 'Of Jakesham' 12 names are shown, the first is:

Thomas le Neweman of Jakesham holds 15 acres for 2s 8d equably, and gives a hen and five eggs: And he shall do three boon works in harvest and give tallage, childwit and fine for his daughters as above.

Most of the other entries end with 'and by the same customs as the aforesaid Thomas'.

The next category is 'Workers holding full lands' and begins with poor Ralph de Humbletoft who had a terribly heavy work load:

Ralph de Humbletoft holds a virgate of land which contains 24a and gives 1d of hedernewech at Xmas and a hen at the same term, and 10 eggs at Easter. And he owes from the feast of St Michael to the gule of August; every week, two works, and from the gule of August to the feast of St. Michael, every week, 5 works, with food if he works for the whole day or without food for half a day. And be it known that he shall not be quit of any work on account of any feast during the year, except during the 12 days of Xmas and during all festal days in harvest. And be it known that he shall plough between the feast of St Michael and the feast of All Saints 1a without food and a work of graserthe by custom. And from the feast of All Saints until the lord's corn shall be quite sown he shall plough in like manner by custom ½ acre every week for one work the 12 days of Xmas excepted as above. And moreover for the ploughing of every ½a he shall have 6 barley loaves, such as (unreadable). 216 loaves ought to be made from 1 quarter. And if it shall happen that he cannot plough on some day in the week owing to frost, then he shall be quit of that ploughing but in the same week for default of that ploughing he shall do one other work: And be it known that whatever he has reploughed in the year or ploughed for sowing he shall harrow without food, and work except at one boon work of the plows which is called 'lovebene' at which he ought not to harrow, but he shall come to that boon work with his plow, or with so many (oxen) as he yokes at the lord's food, namely bread, ale, meat and chees or eggs: and be it known that no one shall come on that day at the lord's food except those only who have been working in the field: and if he has not a beast to be yoked, then he shall come with his sedleph to the field to sow or with his horse, the which if he has, to harrow.

Item, he shall cart the lord's muck for half a day once in the year by custom, from morning until the none hour without food and a work: and if it shall be necessary to cart more muck then he shall cart until the none hour with cart, two horses and two men but it shall be all-owed to him for the ploughing of half an acre: and he shall have for this six loaves as above. And as often as there shall be need he shall spread muck from morning until the none hour or (over) one rig and a half for a work. And similarly he shall weed from morning until the none hour for a work: and he shall find a man to spred, toss, gather and cock hay in the meadow from morning until the none hour for a work but he shall not mow the hay he shall carry. And he shall find a man reaping in harvest or working in another way every work-day except Saturday, from morning until the none hour for a work or for the whole day for a work with food. And at each of the three boon works of harvest he shall find in like manner a man reaping at the lord's food with water viz at bread and one dish of meat, fish, herring or codfish, with one of his peers; and at the fourth boon work he shall find a man reaping at the lord's food in the same way as at the boon works of the ploughing as above: and as often as there is need he shall carry the lord's corn with his cart in harvest with two horses and one, his man, who ought to reap for him on that day in the field, through the whole day with food for one work or through the half day for one work without food. And he shall thatch the straw from morning until the none hour for a work or through the whole day for a work with food. And he shall thresh 24 sheaves of wheat or winter corn, or 40 sheaves of barley or oats outside harvest or beans or peas from morning until the none hour for a work but he shall not winnow. And he shall come with his horse to the lord's grange for three quarters of barley and thereof he shall make malt and shall bring it back to the grange without food and a work, or he shall give for that 2d. And he shall give pannage viz for every pig above a year old 1d and for every sow ½d and for every hog worth 5½d. And he shall give faldage viz for every ox 1d and for every cow with calf 2d and for every sterile cow 1d and for every young beast of two years ½d and for five sheep 1d; and thus neither his sheep nor other cattle ought to lie in the lord's fold. And he shall fence 12 perches round the park and 12 perches round Toftwode and 2 perches round the court without food and a work; and he shall cut and carry all the brush-wood for fencing all the perches but he shall have the old hedges. And he shall make journey out of harvest yearly both short and long with a cart or with horse and sack. The short to Schypedham, Helmham, Hokering, and [places] similar to these and each journey shall be allowed him for a work. The long with horse and sack, to Bregham, Brandon Bridge, Feltewell, Northwande, Hocwande, Rondeshil without Lenn, Norwic, Schenefelde towards Pulham and to similar places for a work. And if he should make a long journey with a cart, then he and four others, his peers, shall find a cart with four horses for the same places aforesaid without food, but it shall be allowed to each of them for a work. And if he shall make that journey in harvest, then he shall be quit of his harvest works by so much time as he was on that journey on a festival in or out of harvest it shall nevertheless be allowed to him for a work. And he ought to dig in the turbary or without, to dyke and bank ditches [and] fishponds, or to cleanse the pools, to roof houses, to stop hedges, to wash and shear sheep and to do other irregular and small jobs for his work from morning to the none hour for a work, or for the whole day for a work with food, or for two works without food. And he owes suit of the mills and shall give tallage at the lord's will and childwit for his daughters if they be incontinent with anyone and have children, and fine for marrying his sons and daughters. And if he be sick within harvest or without, it shall be allowed him for nothing and if he die, then his heir shall make fine with the lord for the heriot, viz 20s or as best he can but the wife of the same deceased shall have the half of his land for her life and immediately both shall begin to work. The same holds a certain pightell of land for 1¼d yearly, viz at the feast of St Michael ½d and at each of the other terms ½d.

There are 17 names under this heading, most of whom are recorded as 'holds the land in the same manner, like as the aforesaid Ralph'.

Those holding half full lands were expected to do much the same work as those holding full lands except John, son of Robert who

> Holds half a virgate of land in the same manner: or he shall make the ironwork of two ploughs annually and the lord shall find the iron and steel; and he shall have every year a tree of the price of 18d. And he shall plough ½ acre of custom without food or a work as above. And from the feast of All Saints he shall plough until the barley is all sown 1 acre every week as above. And he shall fence 12 perches round the Park as above and 12 perches round Toftwode and 2 round the Court. The same holds 17 acres for 5s 10d equably.

There were 12 names under this heading.

The next heading is 'Of workers holding six acres of land' and lists 15 names, followed by one name under 'Of those holding four acres of land'.

Details under the last two categories 'Of those new infeofed' and 'Of the Market' we have given in full in view of their special interest. Most of these holdings are too small for a family to live off and are no doubt premises in the town. It suggests a thriving community is forming round the market and the new white church, with many of the tenants bearing names suggestive of their trades, Smith, Turner, Baker. Vintner, Taylor, etc., We even had a doctor, Master Ralph the Physician, who paid 4d. rent for his surgery. But here are the details from which you can draw your own conclusions and perhaps decide what Roger Cristemasse did with the wall for which he paid ¼d. every Michaelmas Day, and what the dickstede held by William Ede was.

> Of those New infeofed.
>
> Richard Langly holds 4a for 12d equably.
> Geoffrey de Corstone holds 3a for 10d equably.
> Robert le Despenser holds 11½a for 23d equably.
> Robert, son of Matthew de Humbeltoft holds 9a for 2s 4d equably.
> Margaret and Lecia, daughters of William le Mon hold a messuage for 2d equably.
> Walter son of Nicholas holds 6a of land for 18d equably.
> Ralph le Man holds ½a for 2d equably.
> Richard Dive holds a messuage outside the market, towards the east, for 2d equably.
> Osbert Coyteman holds a place behind his messuage, towards the east, for 5¾d.
> Richard atte Forthe holds a place behind his messuage, towards the east, for 5¾d.
> Andrew de Akre holds a place behind his messuage, towards the east, for 8d equably.
> Alexander le Teynturer holds a place behind his messuage, towards the east, for 12d equably.
> Ranulph son of Ralph holds a place behind his messuage, towards the east for 6¼d.
> Mabel [daughter] of Osebert holds a place behind her messuage, towards the east, for 6d and half a farthing.
> William le Glenman holds a place there for 6d and half a farthing.
> Nigel le Turner holds a place behind his messuage, towards the east, for 9d equably and ¼d.
> Henry Cresenben holds a place behind his messuage, towards the east, for 9¼d.
> Gila daughter of Vincent holds a place behind her messuage, toward the east, for 5¼d.
> Walter le Poter holds a place behind his messuage, towards the east, for 9¾d
> Alexander Sywate holds a place behind his messuage, towards the east, for 6¼d.
> John Lovat holds a place behind his messuage, towards the east, for 6¼d.
> William and Adam, bakers, hold a place behind their messuage, towards the east, for 6¼d.

Matthew the clerk holds a place behind his mesuage, towards the east, for 18d equably.

Henry the Vintner holds a mesuage and 7a 1r for 3s 6d yearly equably, by the charter of Bishop Hugh who now is.

Robert Juket holds a certain wall for ¼d at the feast of St Michael.

Robert Ruter holds a certain purpresture for 1d at the feast of St Andrew and at the Nativity of St John.

Thomas Brythwy holds a certain purpresture for 1d at the same terms.

William de Rohawe holds a place behind his mesuage, towards the east, for 8¼d.

Alexander Langly holds a place behind his mesuage, towards the east, for 12½d.

Geoffrey le Taylur holds a place behind his mesuage, towards the east, for 4d equably and ¾d.

Symon Treye holds a place behind his mesuage, towards the east, for 6d equably.

Ralph Pulman holds a place behind his mesuage, towards the east, for 2d equably.

Adam the Smith (Faber) holds a mesuage for 6s equably by the lord's Court.

The same holds a mesuage with a smithy for 12d equably.

Henry le Porter holds a place by the Court for 3s 6d equably.

John le Stynor holds a place there for 3s 6d equably.

Alexander le Barkere holds a place there for 18d equably.

Maurice the Smith (Faber) holds a mesuage for 20d equably.

William Dunecan holds a mesuage for 2s equably.

Master Ralph the Physician (medicus) holds a mesuage for 4d equably.

Richard the Vintner holds a certain place with the old Toll House for 2s 4d.

Robert the Smith holds two places of land for 5s equably.

William de Dockynge and Berta his wife hold 1a for 2d equably.

John Frere holds five little mesuages for 18d equably.

Adam de Bridewell holds a mesuage for 12d equably.

Ralph son of Vincent holds a pightle of land by his mesuage for ½d.

Richard Starling hold a certain pightle of land for ½d at the feast of St Michael.

William Ede holds a dickstede for 1d at the feast of St Michael.

The Parson holds a mesuage which was Geoffrey Starling's, in ex change, for 4d yearly, equably.

Edrich holds a tongue (languetta) of land for ½d at the feast of St John. Reyner de Suthwode holds a certain wall for ½d yearly.

William le Harpur holds 5a for 8d equably.

Roger Cristemass holds a certain wall for ¼d yearly at the feast of St Michael.

Of the Market.

Matthew Clerk (clericus) holds a mesuage for 14d equably and three boon works in harvest.

Lecencia Fisk holds a mesuage for 13d equably and three boon works in harvest.

Alice daughter of William le Mon holds a mesuage for 4d equably and ½d.

Alexander Mus holds a mesuage for 4½d equably.

Symon de Bradenham holds a mesuage for 4½d equably.

Walter the Poter holds a mesuage for 4d equably.

William de Massingham and Gila hold a mesuage for 9d equably.

Richard, son of Matthew, holds two mesuages for 13½d equably.

Geoffrey Clerk holds three mesuages for 13d equably which were Adam Chaplain's (capellani) and Matilda's.

Robert le Despenser holds three mesuages which were Adam Humbeltoft's for 9d equably.

Richard ate Forthe and Abba his wife hold a mesuage for 4½d.

Item, Geoffrey Clerk (clericus) holds a mesuage which was Ralph Springald's for 4½d.

Alexander le Teinturer holds two mesuages which were Albin's for 13d equably.

Osbert Coyteman holds a mesuage which was Richard Albin's for 4½d equably.

Item, Geoffrey Clerk holds a place which was Ordmer's and Matilda his wife's for ½d at the feast of St Andrew.

Ralph Pinchehale holds a mesuage for 4d equably.

Martin Neve holds a shed for 2d equably.

Henry Vinter holds a certain smithy (fabricam) for 4d equably and ¼d.

Ralph Palman holds a little mesuage for ½d at the feast of St Andrew.

Item, Alexander le Teynturer holds a tenter ground for 1d yearly, equably.

And be it known that every anilepman shall give yearly for chevage 1d at the feast of St Michael. And they are worth yearly 3s and sometimes more sometimes less.

And be it known that the lord, if he wishes, can make his Reeve of any molman holding at least 12a of land or of any worker holding a virgate of land, or, at least, half a virgate. And then that molman who shall be Reeve shall be quit of all his annual rent and of all his customs for the year. And he shall have his food from the gule of August unto the feast of St Michael. And if one holding one or half a virgate of tillable land shall be Reeve, then he shall be quit of all his annual rent and of all his customs and works; and he shall have his food in the manner abovesaid. And he shall have forage for his horse in winter and chaff (paleam) as often as he comes riding to the Court for the Business of the Bishop.

Also, be it known that the lord, if he wishes, can make his Beadle of any molman holding at least 6a of land, or of any worker holding 6a. And then he shall be quit of all his rent of assize and of his customs and works. And in summer he may have his horse in the ways, marlpits and fields and in the old dikes outside the Park, and his food in harvest as the reeve.

Also be it known that the lord, if he wishes, can make his Forester of any molman of his holding at least 6a of land. And then he shall be quit of all his customs, and nevertheless he shall give his annual rent of assize. Sum of the whole rent of assize yearly—22li. 2s. 6d. at the four usual terms,

viz:

At the term of St Michael 109s 8¾d.

At the term of St Andrew, similarly.

At the term of Annunciation 108s 11½d.

At the term of St John 114s 1d

Sum of the rent of the Market yearly, 10s 6½d at the four terms equably, but at the feast of St Andrew ½d more.

Sum of Hedernewech yearly with the Reeve and Beadle—2s 6½d at Nativity.

Sum of the Faldage yearly—12s 0½d, sometimes more and sometimes less according to the quantity of animals. And it is at Pentecost with the Reeve and Beadle.

Sum of the Pannage yearly—5s. 6d. with the aforesaid Reeve and Beadle and sometimes more, sometimes less according to the number of pigs.

Sum of the Malting yearly with the aforesaid Reeve and Beadle—57 seams without food and works. And if the lord shall not require that malting, than it is worth in money—3s 2d.

Sum of the journeys with horses of the molmen yearly—67; or they shall give 2d for each: And then the sum will be in money—11s 2d.

Sum of the foot journeys yearly—68; or they shall give 1½d: And then the sum will be in money—8s 6d.

Sum of the plowing of Graserthe yearly of custom and without food and works — 24a—and the ploughing of each acre is worth 4d. Sum in money for that ploughing —8s.

Sum of the ploughing of the custom of molmen yearly without food and works — 91a 3r—or they shall give for the ploughing of each acre 5d with food. And then the sum will be in money—40s 0¾d: or for the ploughing of each acre 4d without food: And then the sum in money will be—32s 5d.

Sum of the ploughing of works yearly which is called Wercherthe with food and allowance of works—292½a—by the small hundred or they shall give for the ploughing of each acre 5d with food and a work: And then the sum will be— 4li 8s 6½d. or for the ploughing of each acre 4d without food and a work: And then the sum will be—58s 6d.

Sum of the harvest boon works yearly—462—by the small hundred. And each boon work is worth 1d. Sum in money for the same boon works —38s 6d.

Sum of the fencing round the Park yearly—741 perches, and round Toftwode—682 perches 1½ feet. And round the Court—68 perches. And the sum total is— 1,491 perches 1½ feet—by the small numeration without food and a work.

Sum of the hens yearly with the Reeve and Beadle—156 hens at Nativity.

Sum of the eggs yearly with the Reeve and Beadle—four hundred, five score and sixteen at Easter.

Sum of the works yearly—four thousand five hundred and twenty three —by the small numeration. And each work in the first month of harvest is worth 1d. And each work in the following fortnight 3¾d. And each work during the other days of harvest ½d. And each work outside harvest is worth ¼d.

Glossary

Advowson	The right to present an incumbent.
Anilepman	A landless tenant of a villein.
Chevage	Payment for living outside the manor but retaining lands.
Childwit	Payment for the right to give a villein's daughter in marriage.
Demesne	The land which the lord of the manor worked or had worked for him.
Fee	A territorial unit nominally held in return for military service.
Foldage	A payment which exempted tenants' sheep and cattle from being folded with those of their lord over the demesne acres.
Free Warren	The right of hunting of beasts and fowls.
Graserthe	A ploughing service in exchange for grazing rights.
Hedernewech	The service of guarding crops.
Molman	The holder of tenancy intermediate between free and customery.
Pightell (Pightle)	A strip in an open field which had been in grass and enclosed for a variable length of time.
Place	This may have been a small enclosed pasture.
Sedleph	Box or basket used by sower for carrying seed.
Stot	A young ox.
Tallage	A payment annually on the land and chattels of a tenant, often at the will of the lord.
Turbary	Usually a place where peat is dug, but here it seems to be used for any common ground.

Appendix V

Memorabilia

This appendix is in the form of a diary of events, news items, etc., concerning Dereham in the 19th century; some repetition from a previous chapter is inevitable; some of the quotes are important, some trivial, but all, we hope, are interesting.

1800

The first news-worthy item of the century appeared in the *Norfolk Chronicle* of 3 May:

> Yesterday se'nnight died at East Dereham in this county the celebrated poet William Cowper, Esq., of the Inner Temple, author of 'The Task' and many other beautiful productions. This amiable and very interesting character was born at Gt. Berkhampstead in Hertfordshire November 15th 1731. His father, the Rector of that parish was John Cowper DD, nephew to the Lord High Chancellor Cowper, and his mother was Ann, daughter of Roger Donne, Gent., late of Ludham Hall in this county.

1801

The first national census taken. Population of Dereham—2,505.

1802

Barker of Dereham is advertising

> Anti-impetigines at £1.13. 0d. per bottle also Whiteheads essence of mustard (a certain remedy for chilblains) at 2s.9d. per bottle.

1803

Birth of George Borrow.

> On an evening of July, in the year 18—, at East D—, a beautiful little town in a certain district of East Anglia, I first saw the light.
>
> *Lavengro*

1804

> March 5th, The East Dereham Loyal Volunteer Cavalry, Capt. Crisp, received their colours, presented by Mrs. Smyth in the names of the ladies of Dereham and neighbourhood.
>
> *Norfolk Annals*
>
> Free loyal Yeomanry, thy country's pride,
> Such as no realm on earth can boast beside,
> Behold thy standard, gift of lady fair,
> No sordid hands could form a work so rare.

1805

> Black Fireaway will cover at Dereham on Fridays this season at 1 guinea and a half the mare and half-a-crown the groom.
>
> *Norfolk Chronicle*

1806

George Thomas (vicar) died. Charles Hyde Wollaston became vicar.

1807

Barker of Dereham is advertising:

> Dr Steer's opodeldoc—cures rheumatism, spasms, palsies, cramps, bruises, sprains, burns, scalds, cuts and stings.

1808

> July 16th—The thermometer has been higher this week than probably was ever noticed in this climate. On Tuesday it was 88, on Wednesday 94 and on Thursday 92. Many horses have died this week from the intense heat of the atmosphere—including a post horse belonging to Mr Bone of Dereham.

> *Norfolk Chronicle*

1809

Proposal that a new fire engine be purchased by the Headboroughs, and a charge of £2.0.0d. be made for its use.

1810

> August 4th—Died Sunday last, in his 73rd year, John Crisp Esq., of East Dereham, who through a long and extensive practice as an Attorney, Clerk to the Magistrates, Commissioners, Deputy Lieutenants etc.,—invariably supported the character of an honest lawyer and eminently useful member of society—being Captain of the East Dereham Yeomanry Cavalry (by wish of the gentlemen composing the troop) his remains will be interred this day with military honours at Shipdham, the place of his nativity.

1811

The census, taken every ten years, showed the population as 2,888. (1,276 males, 1,612 females). There were 551 inhabited and 16 empty houses.

1812

> There will be a public Ball at East Dereham on Tuesday, September 22nd in honour of the Marquis of Wellington's Glorious Victory.
> T.T. Gurdon Esq., Steward.
> Gentlemen's tickets 7/6d each.
> Ladies tickets 3/6d each
> Dancing to begin precisely at 9 o'clock.

1813

November 1st—Death of Lady Fenn, aged 70.

1814

Thursday se'nnight, the return of Peace was celebrated [16 July].

> The morning was ushered in with a merry peal and firing guns. Immediately after Divine Service a grand procession took place with the effigies of John Bull and Bonaparte which were afterwards placed on top of the shambles. At 2 0'clock 1800 poor inhabitants sat down in the Market- place to a most excellent dinner of plum pudding and beef, which was conducted with the greatest regularity.... At five the signal was given to proceed to Neatherd

Moor where the sports immediately commenced which affored considerable diversion to upward of 6000 spectators among whom were an elegant assemblage of the beauty and fashion of the town and neighbourhood whose animating smiles, combined with the fitness of the weather to render the scene truly gratifying. The evening concluded with a bonfire and a grand display of fireworks in the Market-place.

Norfolk Chronicle

1815

The Enclosure Award was published.

1816

One day last week [26 October] as a poor old woman was going past the windmill on Toftwood Common her hat blew off and in attempting to recover it she approached too near the sails, by which her skull was dreadfully fractured. She lingered two days in the greatest agony, when death ended her suffering.

Norfolk Chronicle

1817

On Sunday last [16 August], about 4 o'clock in the afternoon, a fire broke out in the dwelling house of Mr. Mann, farmer, of Scarning, which entirely consumed the same, but by the timely arrival of the engines from Dereham it was prevented from extending to the out-buildings and stack-yard. Great credit is due to a number of persons from Dereham, for their alacrity upon the occasion, amongst whom were several gentlemen whose judicious directions were of essential service.

Norfolk Chronicle

1818

July 20th. The performances of Mr. David Fisher's company in 'the elegant little theatre' at East Dereham terminated on this date 'When the performers assembled on the stage and drank a parting glass and bade farewell of the crowded audience amid shouts of applause'.

Norfolk Annals

This was the Theatre Royal, built in 1815 by David Fisher.

1819

A meeting was held in the Assembly Rooms to consider the best means of obtaining navigation between Dereham and Norwich.

Norfolk Annals

1820

Durrant's Creditors [29 January]

The creditors who have proved their debts under a Commission of Bankruptcy against James Durrant, late of East Dereham, Innkeeper, may receive a first and final dividend of 4/4d in the pound on the amount of their respective debts any day after the 31st January instant, at Messrs. Gurneys Bank, Norwich. J.S.Parkinson, Solicitor.

Norfolk Chronicle

1821

Census—population 3,244—(1546 males, 1698 females)—630 inhabited, 11 empty houses.

1822

Positively Lee Sugg's last tour in Norfolk—Saturday 14th September at East Dereham. The truly original Mr Lee Sugg and the Precepter of Mathews at Home. At the English Opera House. Who will display his wonderful versality of Talent as the Original Professor and Practical Teacher of The Ventriloquist. From whom many popular Characters of the present day have received their Instructions but the Veteran Actor is happy yet to say that his Pupils, though successful with the Public in some parts, still they have a great deal to learn before they can cope with him As an Actor of all Work Who will on this occasion divide his Truly Novel Entertainments calculated for Rubbing off the Rust of Care, or a Pill to Banish Melancholy—into five acts, viz:

Recitations, Songs, Oratory, Conjuring and Internal Elocution. In which singular and pleasing display of the Human Voice the Performer conveys the sound to various distances from his person, also under hats, glasses, into Cupboards, Closets, Chimneys, under the floor of the place of Performance, outside of the door, of which he will finally make his voice appear as if conversing with some Invisible Being. No person can discover the least motion of his Lips, or Muscles although holding close to his mouth a Burning Candle.

Norfolk Chronicle

1823

Sale by Auction.

Toft Wood Mill Farm, E. Dereham, by Henry Catton on Monday September 29th, 1823. All the valuable Farming Stock, Implements in Husbandry, Dairy and Brewing Utensils, Household Furniture and other effects of the late Mr Robert Norton, deceased, as expressed in Catalogues to be had on Friday the 26th instant, at the principal Inns in the neighbourhood and the Auctioneer, East Dereham. There being upward of 200 lots, the Sale will commence precisely at 11 o'clock.

Norfolk Chronicle

1824

Ten Pounds Reward.

Whereas on Friday night last or early on Saturday morning, some person or persons did enter the premises of Mr Henry Andrews, on Neatherd's Moor and steal therefrom a Bay Mare, about 14 hands high, four black legs, off leg behind swelled, and a white mark against the tail where the crupper goes. Whoever will give information of the Offender or Offenders, so as he or they may be brought to Conviction—shall receive a reward of Five Pounds from the East Dereham Town Association and a further reward of Five Pounds from the said Henry Andrews.

1825

In his Will Wm. Taylor bequeathed £250 to distribute bread to the deserving poor every 21 December. Parson Armstrong often mentions distributing loaves on St Thomas's day—sometimes as many as 400.

1826

East Dereham—New Association for the prevention of crime and for prosecuting offenders. A meeting of the members of this association will be held at the Assemby Rooms, East Dereham on Friday 28th day of July instant at 12 o'clock, when the Treasurers accounts will be audited and the Members present will proceed to the Election of a Treasurer and Solicitor in the room of Mr R.W. Palmer deceased and transact such other business as may be found necessary. A full attendance of the members is particularly requested.   By order of the Committee

East Dereham, 18th July, 1826.

1827

Committed to the Castle (by the Rev. Wm Girling) John Brooke, charged on the oath of Richard Carter of East Dereham, with having stolen a silver spoon, his property, and Daniel Roach, for receiving the same, well knowing it to be stolen.

1828

Death of Dr. William Hyde Wollaston, 'The most illustrious of Dereham's sons in the world of chemistry and Natural Philosophy'.

1829

17th December—Death of James Philo, Parish Clerk.

> Well, Peace to thee, thou fine old chap,
> despiser of dissenters and hater of papists,
> as became a dignified and high-church clerk.

Lavengro

1830

On Monday last a Coroner's inquest was held at East Dereham on the body of John Allen, who on the preceding Saturday was driving a brewery dray when one of the horses took fright and in attempting to turn him, the animal plunged and knocked the unfortunate man down, when the wheel passed over his body and he survived but a few hours. Verdict, accidental death with a deodand of 1/- on the dray.

1831

The census showed the town's population had grown to 3,919.

1832

Death of David Fisher the elder. He was buried in Dereham churchyard; the funeral by all accounts being very grand. The carriages sent by the neighbouring gentry formed a procession a quarter of a mile in length.

1833

March 30th. This day is published in a neat pocket volume, the East Dereham collection of Psalm Tunes arranged for the piano forte or organ. The second edition, revised and corrected—Price 3/6d neatly bound. Published by H. Barker.

1834

Theatre, Dereham.

The bespeak of the Hon. Mr and Mrs Milles, on Wednesday se'nnight [26 July] produced, as might be expected (although we regret to say that it was one of the novelties of the season) a full house. The performances were *Pedlar's Acre*, with the interlude of *Mischief Making* and the farce of *Teddy the Tyler* in all of which pieces the comic powers of Mr C Fisher Jnr. convulsed the house with laughter, notwithstanding the melting countenances of many who could not resist the effects of the heat of the weather. Miss Morgen is a pleasing singer and a very clever actress, nor must we omit to notice Miss Hayes who, though new to the boards, promises to be an acquisition to the company. Her countenance and figure are prepossessing and her voice melodious. We sincerely hope, as the season is drawing to a conclusion, that the exertions of this highly respectable company will be more productive than they have been hitherto.

Norfolk Chronicle

1835

The building of the Gas Works commenced, This stood in Quebec Road, and was the first step in introducing the technology of the Industrial Revolution into this formerly pastoral town.

1836

To be sold by Auction by Mann & Clarke at the *George Inn*, East Dereham on Friday 10th June next at 6 o'clock. All that newly erected and substantially built Brick Tower windmill eligibly situate within ten minutes walk of the Market Place of East Dereham comprising five floors and driving two pair of stones, with capability of adding a third pair, with patent sails, winding herself, iron shaft, flour mill, jumper, sack tackling and all other necessary machinery on the latest and most improved principles, with stable and cart lodge and about one acre and three quarters of excellent Freehold land adjoining, of all of which Immediate Possession may be had. Apply to Mr Wm. Drake, Solicitor. East Dereham, to Messrs Beckwith and Dye, Solicitors, Norwich, to Mr Michael or James Hardy, the Proprietors on the Premises or to the Auctioneers, East Dereham or at their offices 73 St Stephens Street, Norwich.

This mill, situated in Cherry Drift, was known at that time as Fendick's Mill, and has now been refurbished and opened as a museum.

1837

Swindling—a new way [18 March]

A boy is travelling the county visiting Inns and Public Houses where he plays off tricks of dexterity of hand for the amusement of the company during which he frequently borrows a sovereign for the purpose and during his hocus-pocus operations, contrives to exchange the good coin for a counterfeit one. The arch rogue repeated this trick twice in one house in Dereham a few days ago.

Norfolk Chronicle

1838

Eagle Family and Commercial Inn.
East Dereham, Norfolk.

William Cowper

Begs to inform the Nobility, Gentry and Public that he has taken the above Inn and trusts by assiduity and attention, to merit a portion of their favours. Commercial Gentlemen may confidently rely upon their comforts being personally attended to. Wines and Spirits of the finest quality.

Norfolk Chronicle

1841

Census—population now 3,834.

1843

The manor of Oldhall and Syricks was bought by George Cooper for 1,000 guineas.

1844

August 28th—A shocking accident occurred at Dereham Theatre to Mr Dillon, one of the perfomers. He had just dressed for his part and approached too near a lighted candle, the inflammable material which he wore immediately caught fire and he was enveloped in flames. He ran about the stage in terror, and some of the audience rushing forward, endeavoured to extinguish the fire, but they did not succeed until he had been seriously injured.

Norfolk Annals

1845

There were 50 public gas lamps in Dereham by this date.

1846

Jeremiah William Gidney built St Nicholas Ironworks. 'The Iron Foundry of Mr Gidney is an establishment equal in point of mechanical ingenuity to those of Sheffield and Birmingham; a curious and elegant article termed the strained invisible wire fencing is manufactured here.'

Hunt's *Directory*, 1850

1847

The Wymondham—Dereham Railway was opened for passenger traffic.

1848

The King's Lynn—Dereham Railway opened.

1849

The Dereham—Fakenham Railway opened.

1850

The Rev. B.J. Armstrong appointed vicar.

1851

The census showed a population of 4,385. The size of the town was steadily increasing, to the detriment of the surrounding villages.

1852

Death of W.W. Lee-Warner of Quebec Hall. 'His noble, generous nature ever keenly alive to the wants of his fellow creatures whom he relieved with no sparing hand'.

1853

Opening of the Mechanics' Institute. The event was recorded with relish by Parson Armstrong since he had been a prominent member of the organizing committee.

> November 9th—A day of much interest among the artizans of Dereham in consequence of the inaugural lecture of the Institute—Lord Sondes, president, accompanied by his daughters the Misses Milles. 297 persons attended, The lecturer was the Rev. Bath Power of Norwich, subject 'Physical science, on its relation to the Arts and conveniences of Life'—Mr Power gave and interesting exhibition of the Electric Telegraph'.

The Institute soon became an important part of the town's social life.

1854

Capt. W.E.G. Lytton-Bulwer of Quebec Hall wounded at the Battle of Alma in the Crimea.

1855

On 18 May Capt. Lytton-Bulwer received the Crimea Medal from the hands of Her Majesty. On 5 July he married Miss Lee-Warner.

1856

On 29 May a public Thanksgiving for Peace was held (the end of the Crimea War). All schools in Dereham had a 'Grand tea-drinking' in the Market-place, followed by fireworks. About 600 sat down and afterwards repaired to the moor for games.

1857

The Corn Hall was opened on 11 February. On 19 July its owners were indicted for obstructing Lion Hill and Quebec Street.

1858

The Attorney General confirmed judgment that the Corn Hall should not be demolished.

1859

Mr H.C. Wigg, late of Dereham gave a lecture on his experiences of seven years in Australia.

1860

'F' Company, 3rd Volunteer Battalion, Norfolk Regiment embodied to meet threat of invasion by Napoleon III. This was another organisation which was soon to play a prominent part in the town's social life.

1861

Census—population 4,368.

1862

The Norfolk Agriculture Show was held in Dereham for the first time.

1863

July 16th—A fire at the premises of William Hubbard, builder, caused damage amounting to £2,000. Arson was suspected.
On August 10th the townspeople met to organise a fire brigade.

1864
Lord Suffield reviewed the Battalion of Volunteers. The Lynn, Holt, Fakenham, Swaffham, Aylsham and other companies joining at Dereham for the day.

1865
The Prince and Princess of Wales came to Dereham by train. They were met by Lord Suffield and Lord Hamilton. The town was lavishly decorated, Triumphal arches were erected and flowers festooned everwhere. Guns were fired and bells rung. The Royal party departed for Gunton by coach.

1866
The Prince and Princess of Wales, Her Majesty the Queen of Denmark and the Duke of Edinburgh arrived by special train on their way to Costessey Park. The Volunteers formed a guard of honour.

1867
January 10th—'The gayest week, perhaps, ever known in Dereham'. The Volunteers gave two theatrical representations, the bachelors gave a Ball, and there was the annual distribution of prizes to the Volunteers.

1868
The Volunteers in camp at Hunstanton Park.

1869
The Norfolk County Cricket Club closed their Dereham ground, which was taken over by the Dereham club.

1870
January 11th—The ladies of Dereham gave a large juvenile party at the Assembly Room at which was a large Christmas tree loaded with toys.

1871
Census—population 5,107.

1872
October 1st—Death of the Rev. W.C.Wollaston—last of the sinecure rectors. His death ended a two-hundred-year association of the Wollaston family with the parish, which had begun when Francis Wollaston bacame rector in 1761.

1873
August 16th—The clock tower of the Church was struck by lightning, 'the electric fluid having passed from top to bottom, shivering the clock wire and preventing its striking'.

1874

The Cowper Congregational Church erected.

1875

Board schools at Etling Green and Toftwood erected, at a cost of £600 and £700 respectively.

1876

February 15th—The Rev.B.J. Armstrong gave supper to the officers and men of the Volunteers at the King's Arms. Captains Upcher and Bulwer, Lieutenants Norgate, Hyde and Barwell and Surgeon Hastings were present.

1877

The parish was constituted into a local government district and the first Board elected.

October 6th—The famous Joseph Arch 'was thundering away in the Corn Hall' (Armstrong's comment).

1879

September 10th—A collision occurred between a dog-cart being driven very fast and a donkey-carriage being driven by the Churchwarden returning from the annual Temperance Tea.

1880

St Withburga Church opened on April 20th. Water Works completed.

1881

Census—population 5,563, but this included a number of navvies employed on the sewage works.

1882

The 'Round-the-World' railway line from Dereham to Norwich via Reepham and Aylsham opened.

1883

Boom time at the Post Office! Parcel Post was introduced, 3 wall letter boxes had been provided; at the railway station, Norwich Road and High Street; and the weekly number of postal items for delivery was 33,326.

1884

Dereham Town Football Club founded.

1885

The Gas Works was taken over by the local authority and moved to the railway at Yaxham Road.

1886

September 9th—Charles Wright, solicitor, buried. He was a famous cricketer and played for Norfolk.

1887

Queen Victoria's Golden Jubilee. A dinner was held in the market place, which was hurdled off at the *King's Arms* at one end and from the pump to the Eagle at the other. Members of the 3rd V.B.N.R. helped to wait, and their band, conducted by Tom Cranmer, was in attendance.

1888

The Rev. B.J. Armstrong resigned due to ill-health—he was replaced by the Rev. H.J.L. Arnold.

1889

Mr. J.J. Wright opened a cycle shop. This was the humble beginning from which grew a thriving business as a motor vehicle, tractor and farm implement agent, one of the town's major businesses.

1890

Death of the much-loved Rev. B.J. Armstrong.

1891

Census—population 5,524.

1892

The Post Office was built in the market place.

1893

The Swimming Pool and Public Baths opened in Bath Avenue. Richard Mayes was the builder and proprietor, and the opening ceremony was performed by Col. Bulmer, with the Temperance Brass Band in attendance. According to a local diarist of that time 'he (Mr.Mayes) could not make them pay so he turned them into 4 houses known as Bath Houses. The balcony at this end was where they used to dive from. The first house in the row was an engine house for heating the bath, etc.'

1894

Dereham Urban District Council formed.

1895

The Recreation Ground was opened by Col. Hyde. Our local diarist (a Mr Farrow) recorded that 'a balloon and parachute went up from the Rec.' He did not record the date but mentioned that the descending parachutist missed the Rec. and landed in a turnip field on the other side of the road.

1896

The Summer Show of the Norfolk Agriculture Association opened. It was a two-day event.

1897

Queen Victoria's Diamond Jubilee. A dinner was held in the market place for 3,100 poor people.

1899

Mr J.J. Wright bought his first motor vehicle. There was a fiery end to the century, when in December the Free Trade House, in Swaffham road caught fire, causing damage estimated at £2,500.

EAST DEREHAM.

Particulars and Conditions of Sale

OF

FREEHOLD

SHOPS & DWELLING-HOUSES,

BUSINESS PREMISES,

COTTAGES AND BLACKSMITH'S SHOP,

VALUABLE FREEHOLD BUILDING SITES & GARDEN GROUNDS,

SMALL ENCLOSURES OF LAND,

AND

14 Shares in the East Dereham Corn Exchange Co.,

WHICH

W. Vincent & F. W. Beck

Who are jointly concerned, on this occasion, are favoured with instructions from the Mortgagees and Executors of the late Mr. W. T. Gidney, TO SELL BY AUCTION,

AT THE KING'S ARMS HOTEL, EAST DEREHAM,

On WEDNESDAY, APRIL 14th, 1897,

AT THREE O'CLOCK PRECISELY.

IN THIRTY-FIVE LOTS.

Particulars and Conditions of Sale may be obtained of the Vendors' Solicitors,

MESSRS. COZENS-HARDY & JEWSON,
Castle Chambers, Norwich,

AND

MESSRS. FRANCIS & BACK,
22, St. Giles' Street, Norwich,

and of the Auctioneers, Mr. W. VINCENT, 11, Upper King Street, Norwich, and Mr. F. W. BECK, East Dereham and Fakenham.

J. METCALF, PRINTER, NORWICH.

97 (Left) Poster advertising the sale of Gidney's estate, 1897.

98 (Opposite) Plan of Gidney's estate.

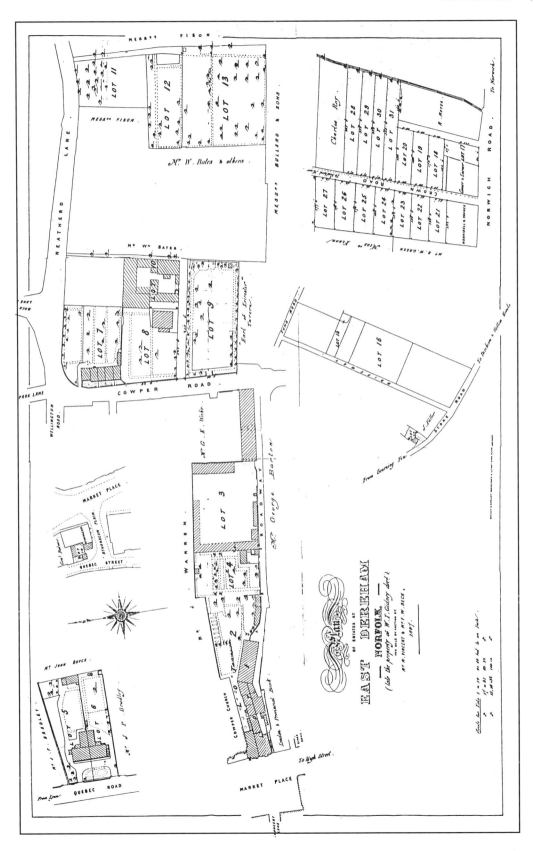

Particulars.

LOT I.

ALL THOSE VALUABLE DOUBLE-FRONTED

SHOP, DWELLING-HOUSE, AND WAREHOUSES

with a Frontage of 23 ft. 9 in. to the Market Place, and comprising IRONMONGER'S SHOP 23 ft. 9 in. by 30 ft. with Private and Clerks' Offices.

The Dwelling-house contains : Kitchen, Scullery, Storeroom, Breakfast Room, and Entrance Hall on Ground Floor. Drawing and Dining Rooms, Storeroom, Nursery, and W.C. on First Floor. Five commodious Bedrooms on Second Floor. There is also a good Cellar. A Warehouse, part of which is Lean-to, over Kitchen, Scullery, and Breakfast Room 48-ft. by 12-ft. Stove Warehouse 26-ft. by 18-ft. A Long Warehouse part of which is Three Stories high, 45-ft. long, and varying in width from 12-ft. to 20-ft. built of Brick and Tiled. Another Warehouse 45-ft. by 20-ft,, Three Stories high, built of Brick and covered with Corrugated Iron. Also the Iron Warehouse 27-ft. by 25-ft. 6ins., which is built of Brick and covered with Corrugated Iron. The whole is known as No. 37, Market Place, East Dereham, is coloured yellow on the Plan, and is occupied by Mr. J. P. Bradley at an apportioned annual rent of £92 10s. 0d. under a Lease for Seven Years from the 6th April, 1894, but determinable by the Lessee, his executors, or administrators, as therein mentioned. A copy of this Lease will be produced at the Auction, and can be inspected at the Office of Messrs. Cozens-Hardy and Jewson before the Sale.

TENURE FREEHOLD.

By an Agreement dated the 10th of November, 1891, and made between The London and Provincial Bank, Limited, of the one part, and William Thomas Gidney of the other part, the Bank agreed to pay the said William Thomas Gidney a rent of 2s. 6d. per annum for an encroachment, and the Bank further agreed within one month after notice given by the said William Thomas Gidney, his heirs, and assigns to remove all projections to the North of the red line shown on the Plan thereto annexed, and that the said William Thomas Gidney, his heirs, and assigns should be at liberty to carry up or re-build his building higher than the Bank premises. This agreement or a copy will be produced at the auction, and can be inspected at the office of Messrs. Cozens-Hardy and Jewson before the auction.

LOT 2.

ALL THAT VALUABLE FREEHOLD

DWELLING-HOUSE AND JEWELLER'S SHOP,

known as No. 36, Market Place, and adjoining Lot 1, built of Brick, and covered with Tile and Slate, containing Shop 14-ft. 6-in. by 15-ft. 3-in., with Bay Window 2-ft. 3-in. deep, Entrance Hall, and Dining Room on Ground Floor. Kitchen, Pantry, and Workshop in Basement. Landings and Two Bedrooms on First Floor. Two Bedrooms on Second Floor. There is also a Wooden Workshop, Greenhouse, Scullery, and Earth Closet with Room over same, and a Large Garden. The whole being splendidly situated and now in the occupation of Mr. W. H. Harris at the annual rent of £50. In addition to the above, there are Two Oil Sheds marked on the Plan A and B now occupied by Mr. J. P. Bradley at an apportioned annual rent of 10/-, under the above mentioned Lease, expiring on the 6th of April, 1901.

Under a verbal arrangement entered into many years since between the Trustees of Cowper Congregational Church and the late Mr. Gidney, the Trustees have enjoyed for more than Twenty Years a right-of-way from the passage on the South side of this Lot across the garden (forming part of this Lot) to the hereditaments belonging to them for the purpose of cleaning windows and gutters, painting and repairing buildings, and taking in coals, in consideration of which the said Mr. W. T. Gidney was permitted to open windows on the North side of the house forming part of this lot, overlooking the front yard of Cowper Congregational Church. This lot will be sold subject to and with the benefit of the right of way and lights mentioned above, and it shall be assumed without question that the Trustees of Cowper Congregational Church and the Vendors have respectively acquired legal rights of way for the purposes aforesaid and of light, and no requisition shall be made as to the origin or existence of such rights.

Possession will be given, except as to the Two Oil Sheds, on completion of purchase.

LOT 3.

ALL THOSE COMMODIOUS

IMPLEMENT STORES AND WORKSHOPS,

situate in Cowper Road, and comprising : Iron Stores and Show Shop, 70-ft. by 24-ft., built of Brick and covered with Corrugated Iron, containing Offices for Principal, Foreman, and Clerk, and the First Floor of which is a Showroom of the same dimensions. Adjoining the above is the Smithy which is built of Brick and Stone and covered with Corrugated Iron, and is 24-ft. 6-in. square, being fitted with Four Forges. The Carpenters' and Wheelwrights' Shop is built of Wood and covered with Corrugated Iron, the dimensions of which are 78-ft. by 17-ft. 6-in. There is also a long range of buildings, forming Drying

Shed, Implement and Carriage Sheds, Paint Shop and Stores, built of Wood and covered with Corrugated Iron and Tiles, as well as a covered Sawpit, Oil House, Tyre Heating Furnace, and Large Yard, and all the convenient arrangements in connection with the manufacture of general Agricultural Implements, Carriages, and Machines. The whole has an area of 0a. 2r. 1p. more or less, and is situate as above, adjoining Lot 4, and is occupied by the Late Mr. W. T. Gidney's Executors. The Erection at the South East Corner marked C to D on the Plan in the occupation of Mr. J. P. Bradley, under the above mentioned Lease at an apportioned rent of 5/- per annum is included in this lot.

TENURE FREEHOLD.

The purchaser of this Lot at the expiration or sooner determination of Mr. Bradley's Lease will have to erect a partition fence between the points marked X and Y on the Plan, and he will in addition to the purchase money have to pay the sum of £130 10s. 0d. for the following Fixtures, *viz.*: all the Iron Hooks on joists in Bottom Show Room, Crane with Endless Chain in Upper Show Room, Self-acting Screw Cutting Lathe, 11-in Gap Lathe, 30-in. Drilling Machine with Back Gear, Punching and Shearing Machine, Six-horse Power Engine and Boiler with Tank, Bench and Drawers, Grindstone and Trough, and all the Shafting in Fitting and Turning Shop, Four Back Stocks and Troughs, Bench and Drawers, Fan and Set of Sheet Iron Rollers in Yard.

Possession will be given, except as to the Erection marked C to D, on completion of Purchase.

LOT 4.

ALL THAT FREEHOLD

GARDEN,

situate between Lots 2 and 3, and containing 0a. 0r. 34½p. in the occupation of Mr. J. P. Bradley under the above mentioned Lease at an apportioned annual rent of £6 15s. 0d., well stocked with choice Fruit Trees and Bushes, and having tastefully laid out Flower Beds and Croquet Lawn.

Standing upon this lot is a Cart Shed and Stable for one Horse, built of Wood and covered with Corrugated Iron, which will be included in the Sale.

LOT 5.

A VALUABLE FREEHOLD

DWELLING-HOUSE,

built of Red and Faced with White Bricks and covered with Slate, containing on the Ground Floor, Entrance Hall, Dining and Drawing Rooms, Kitchen, Scullery, Pantry, Storeroom, and Coal House. On First Floor, Dressing Room, Four Bedrooms, Linen and other Closets, with W.C. on Landing. There is also a good Cellar. The Outbuildings comprise a Brick, Stone, and Slated Stable and Coach House, and Servants' W.C.

The Front is approached by Carriage Drive with small Garden next the road, and in the rear there is a Lawn and Kitchen Garden, and a Cluster of Beech Trees forming a Bower. This lot has a Frontage next Quebec Road of 45-ft., and a depth of 188 ft., and is known as No. 14, and occupied by Mr. John Duncan, who is a yearly tenant, at a rent of £30. Water and Gas are laid on and supplied by the Urban District Council.

LOT 6.

ALL THAT VALUABLE FREEHOLD

DWELLING-HOUSE,

built of Red and Faced with White Bricks, and covered with Tiles, adjoining Lot 5, and containing Rooms of the same size and description as that lot on the Ground Floor, with Five Bedrooms and Dressing Room on First Floor, W.C. on Landing. There is also a Cellar and Back Staircase. There is also a Conservatory with this Lot.

The Front is approached by Carriage Drive with small Garden next Quebec Road, and there is a Lawn and Kitchen Garden at the Back, the whole having a frontage to Quebec Road of 46 ft. 6 ins., is known as No. 12, and is in the occupation of Mr. J. P. Goddard, who is a yearly tenant, at the rent of £32 10s. 0d.

The accommodation in this Lot is almost identical with Lot 5.

Note as to Lots 5 and 6. The owner of the land on the opposite side of the road is restricted by Covenant from erecting any building thereon without the covenant of the owner of these Lots.

LOT 7.

ALL THOSE FOUR FREEHOLD

COTTAGES,

built of Brick and covered with Tiles, situate at the corner of Cowper Road and Neatherd Lane, each containing Two Lower Rooms and Two Bedrooms, with Sheds and Outhouses thereto belonging, together with a Large Garden for each Tenement, well stocked with Fruit Trees and a Well of good water, the whole containing 0a. 1r. 11½p., now occupied by Mr. Murrell and others at the annual rent of £36, and known as Nos. 4, 6, 8, and 10, Cowper Road.

LOT 8.

VALUABLE PIECE OF FREEHOLD

BUILDING LAND,

situate in Cowper Road and adjoining Lots 7 and 10, containing 0a. 1r. 6p. or thereabouts, having a frontage of 92-ft. next Cowper Road, and a depth of 121-ft., two sides of which are enclosed with a Stone Wall 5-ft. high. Part of this Land is occupied by Mr. Ottoway, (who is under notice to quit at Michaelmas,) at an annual rent of £2. There is a Large Range of Wooden Buildings covered with Corrugated Iron, forming Warehouse, Cart Shed, &c., upon this Lot, as occupied by the Late Mr. Gidney's Executors, which will be included in the sale.

The Purchaser of this Lot will have a right to use, free of charge, with or without horses, carts, and carriages, the Roadway adjoining, which will be sold with Lot 10.

Possession of the part of this Lot, occupied by the Late Mr. Gidney's Executors, will be given on completion.

LOT 9.

A VALUABLE PIECE OF FREEHOLD

PASTURE & BUILDING LAND,

with a frontage of 96-ft. next Cowper Road, and a depth of 210-ft., forming a very desirable Building Site, being nicely studded with Timber, which will be included in the Sale, the whole containing 0a. 1r. 32p. or thereabouts, and now occupied by Mr. George Pells, a yearly tenant, (who is under notice to quit at Michaelmas,) at an annual rent of £5.

The Purchaser of this Lot will have a right to use, free of charge, with or without horses, carts, and carriages, the Road separating it from Lots 8 and 10.

The small Brick and Tiled Building on this Lot used as a Powder Magazine belongs to Mr. J. P. Bradley, who has a right to occupy the same, free of rent, until the 11th of October next, and to remove the same any time before such date.

LOT 10.

ALL THAT SUBSTANTIALLY BRICK BUILT AND TILED

MOULDING SHOP,

39-ft. by 23-ft., with Engine House 22-ft- 6-in., by 11-ft. 3-in., Well Lighted Smithy 62-ft. by 23-ft., Lathe and Turning Room 33-ft. by 13-ft., Drying Shed 25-ft. by 13-ft., Warehouse 47-ft. by 25-ft. 6-ins., Three Stalled Stable with Loft over same Coach House, Harness House, Two Loose Boxes, and Coke House, the whole being known as the Foundry, and is situate near Cowper Road, on the East of Lot 8, and was lately in the occupation of Mr. W. T. Gidney's Executors. There is a Well of good water on this Lot.

TENURE FREEHOLD.

The private Roadway leading from Cowper Road, over which the Purchasers of Lots 8 and 9, and other persons have a right-of-way, will be sold with this Lot. The purchaser of this Lot will have a right-of-way over the roadway on the East side of this Lot leading to Neatherd Lane.

The Purchaser of this Lot will have to erect a boundry Fence between the points marked E and F, on the Plan, and will have to pay the sum of £30 0s. 0d. over and above the purchase money for the following Fixtures, viz.: Beam Iron Column, Crane, Cupola, Engine and Boiler, Fan and Shafting, Drilling Machine, Screwing Machine, Bench and Drilling Machine, Three Back Stocks and Troughs, Grindstone and Bench as fixed.

Possession of this Lot will be given on completion.

LOT 11.

A VALUABLE FREEHOLD

BUILDING SITE,

situate in Neatherd Lane, to which it has a frontage of 83-ft. with a depth of 124-ft., and containing 0a. 1r. 13p. more or less, and now occupied as a Garden by Mr. Guymer and Mr. Burleigh, who are under notice to quit at Michaelmas. The purchaser of this Lot will have a right to use the Road on the East side thereof, leading into Neatherd Lane, on the usual terms

A VALUABLE PIECE OF FREEHOLD

LOT 12.

GARDEN GROUND,

situate on the South side of Lot 11, and containing 0a. 0r. 36p., well planted with Fruit Trees, and now occupied by Mr. Burleigh, who is under notice to quit at Michaelmas.

The Purchaser of this Lot will have a right-of-way to use the Road on the East side, leading into Neatherd Lane, on the usual terms.

A VALUABLE PLOT OF FREEHOLD

LOT 13.

GARDEN GROUND,

containing 0a. 2r. 19p. more or less, and situate on the south side of Lot 12, well planted with Fruit Trees and Bushes, with Water laid on and supplied from the Urban District Council Main. The Roadway leading to Neatherd Lane will be sold with this Lot, subject to the right for the purchasers of Lots 11 and 12 to pass over same. This Lot is now occupied by Mr. Wm. Hodgkinson, who is under notice to quit at Michaelmas.

ALL THAT FREEHOLD

LOT 14.

COTTAGE AND BLACKSMITH'S SHOP,

built of Brick and covered with Tiles, containing Two Living Rooms, Three Bedrooms, Two Attics with Blacksmith's Shop and Traves, Lean-to Shed and Back Yard, known as No. 22, Quebec Street, and now occupied by Mr. Brunton, who is under notice to quit at Michaelmas, at the annual rent of £12.

This Lot is well situated and adjoins property belonging to General Bulwer on the North, the Headboroughs on the East, and Quebec Street on the West, as shown on the plan.

A PIECE OF FREEHOLD

LOT 15.

ARABLE LAND,

situate on the Driftway Lane, Toftwood Common, and containing 0a. 0r. 31p. or thereabouts, now in the occupation of Mr. Wm. Copeman, a yearly tenant, (who is under notice to quit,) at the annual rent of 5/-.

AN ENCLOSURE OF FREEHOLD

LOT 16.

ARABLE LAND,

situate in Driftway Lane, Toftwood Common, near Lot 15, and containing 1a. 0r. 7p. or thereabouts, as now occupied by Mr. Wm. Copeman, (who is under notice to quit,) at the annual rent of £1.

A VALUABLE FREEHOLD

LOT 17.

BUILDING SITE,

situate on Norwich Road, adjoining property belonging to Mr. Larner on the West, coloured red on the plan, having a frontage of 60-ft. next Norwich Road, and a depth of 128-ft. 6-ins. or thereabouts, and containing in all 0a. 0r. 27p, in the occupation of Mr. Richard Mayes at an apportioned rent of £0 14s. 6d. per annum.

The purchaser of this Lot will have the right to use the back roadway leading into Crown Road on payment of one quarter of the expenses of keeping the same in repair.

LOT 18.

ALL THAT DESIRABLE AND VALUABLE FREEHOLD

BUILDING SITE,

situate on the East side of Crown Road, with a frontage next same of 60-ft. and a depth of 168-ft., and containing 0a. 0r. 37p. more or less. Occupier, Mr. Richard Mayes. Apportioned rent £0 14s. 6d. per annum.

The Back Road will be conveyed to the Purchaser of this Lot, subject to the right of the Purchaser of Lot 17 and of other adjoining owners to use the same.

LOT 19.

A similar Lot to the above with a frontage of 60-ft. and a depth of 174-ft., and containing 0a. 0r. 39p. more or less. Occupier, Mr. Richard Mayes. Apportioned rent £0 14s. 6d. per annum.

LOT 20.

A similar Lot to the above with a frontage of 60-ft. and a depth of 180-ft., and containing 0a. 1r. 0p. more or less. Occupier, Mr. Richard Mayes. Apportioned rent £0 14s. 6d. per annum.

A VALUABLE FREEHOLD

LOT 21.

BUILDING SITE,

situate on the West side of Crown Road with a frontage of 65-ft. next same and a depth of 152-ft. and containing 0a. 0r. 37p. more or less. Occupier, Mr. Richard Mayes. Apportioned rent £0 14s. 6d. per annum.

LOT 22.

A similar Lot having a frontage of 65-ft. and a depth of 156-ft. and containing 0a 0r. 38p. more or less. Occupier, Mr. Richard Mayes. Apportioned rent £0 14s. 6d. per annum.

LOT 23.

A similar Lot having a frontage of 65-ft. and a depth of 158-ft. and containing 0a. 0r. 38p. more or less. Occupier, Mr. Richard Mayes. Apportioned rent £0 14s. 6d. per annum.

LOT 24.

A similar Lot having a frontage of 73-ft. and a depth of 162-ft. and containing 0a. 1r. 3p. more or less. Occupier, Mr. John Green. Apportioned rent £0 12s. 6d. per annum.

LOT 25.

A similar Lot having a frontage of 73-ft. and a depth of 166-ft. and containing 0a. 1r. 4p. more or less. Occupier, Mr. John Green. Apportioned rent £0 12s. 6d. per annum.

LOT 26.

A similar Lot having a frontage of 73-ft., and a depth of 170-ft. and containing 0a. 1r. 5p. more or less. Occupier, Mr. John Green. Apportioned rent £0 12s. 6d. per annum.

LOT 27.

A similar Lot having a frontage of 73-ft., and a depth of 174-ft., and containing 0a. 1r. 5p. more or less. Occupier, Mr. John Green. Apportioned rent £0 12s. 6d. per annum.

LOT 28.

ALL THAT VALUABLE FREEHOLD

BUILDING SITE,

situate on the East side of Crown Road, and having a frontage next same of 47-ft. 6-ins., a depth of 365-ft., and containing 0a. 1r. 26p. more or less. Occupier, Mr. D. Johnson. Apportioned rent £0 13s. 4d. per annum.

LOT 29.

A similar Lot having a frontage of 47-ft. 6-in., a depth of 358-ft., and containing 0a. 1r. 22p. more or less Occupier, Mr. D. Johnson. Apportioned rent £0 13s. 4d. per annum.

LOT 30.

A similar Lot having a frontage of 47-ft. 6ins., a depth of 354-ft., and containing 0a. 1r. 21p. more or less. Occupier, Mr. D. Johnson. Apportioned rent £0 13s. 4d. per annum.

LOT 31.

A similar Lot having a frontage of 47-ft. 6ins., a depth of 349-ft., and containing 0a. 1r. 20p. more or less. Occupier, Mr. D. Johnson. Apportioned rent £0 13s. 4d. per annum.

LOT 32.

ALL THAT FREEHOLD

COTTAGE AND GARDEN,

situate on Toftwood Common, in the occupation of Mr. John Davey, who is under notice to quit at Michaelmas, and containing Two Sleeping and Two Lower Apartments, Pantry and Outhouses, Built of Brick, Clay Lumps, and Boards, and covered with Tiles, with Large Garden, as now let for the annual rent of £5 10s. 0d.

LOT 33.

Five Shares of £20 each in the East Dereham Corn Hall Company.

LOT 34.

Five ditto.

LOT 35.

Four ditto.

The Purchaser of each of the Lot 11, and Lots 17 to 31, inclusive, shall within six months of the day of the completion of his purchase raise or build Boundary Fences or Walls upon his Lot within the boundary, where marked ⊤ on the Plan.

The tenants of Lots 17 to 31, inclusive, are under notice to quit at Michaelmas next.

It is believed that Lot 14 and Lots 17 to 31, inclusive, are free of land tax. The other Lots are sold subject to land tax. All the Lots are sold subject to tithe rent-charge, and subject to and with the benefit of such rights and easements as legally affect or belong to the same.

The vendors reserve the right to hold an auction upon Lots 3, 5, and 10.

Index